To Jenny and ... y

My heart goes pitter
pat when I think
of Anderson's / thank
you for keeping
a favorite place
shing and perfect!

;)

DISROBED

DISROBED

HOW CLOTHING PREDICTS ECONOMIC CYCLES, SAVES LIVES, AND DETERMINES THE FUTURE

SYL TANG

ROWMAN & LITTLEFIELD
Lanham • Boulder • New York • London

Published by Rowman & Littlefield
A wholly owned subsidiary of The Rowman & Littlefield Publishing Group, Inc.
4501 Forbes Boulevard, Suite 200, Lanham, Maryland 20706
www.rowman.com

Unit A, Whitacre Mews, 26-34 Stannary Street, London SE11 4AB

British Library Cataloguing in Publication Information Available

Library of Congress Cataloging-in-Publication Data

Names: Tang, Syl.
Title: Disrobed : how clothing predicts economic cycles, saves lives, and determines the future / Syl Tang.
Description: Lanham : Rowman & Littlefield Publishing Group, [2017] | Includes index.
Identifiers: LCCN 2017005878 (print) | LCCN 2017008532 (ebook) | ISBN 9781442270992 (cloth : alk. paper) | ISBN 9781442271005 (electronic)
Subjects: LCSH: Clothing and dress—Social aspects.
Classification: LCC GT525 .T36 2017 (print) | LCC GT525 (ebook) | DDC 391—dc23
LC record available at https://lccn.loc.gov/2017005878

♾™ The paper used in this publication meets the minimum requirements of American National Standard for Information Sciences—Permanence of Paper for Printed Library Materials, ANSI/NISO Z39.48-1992.

Printed in the United States of America

CONTENTS

INTRODUCTION

WHAT IF I were to tell you clothing trends predicted the 2016 election?

Right before the 2008 US presidential election, a tremendous number of clothing brands created "educational" clothing: Reebok did a T-shirt with John Maeda on math algorithms. Emperial Nation launched T-shirts related to history, depicting events and figures from the American Civil War, the French Revolution, and the Ottoman Empire. The Ken and Dana line presented jewelry citing landmark legal cases, such as the one behind women's right to vote and *Roe v. Wade*.[1] When Barack Obama was elected, many said it was a return to intellectualism, the triumph of a highly educated law professor over the folksy Everyman campaign of his opponent. Was the nation simply ready for a leader who prized intellect over gut feelings?

Looking at those clothing themes prior to the election, it would certainly seem so.

Embracing apparel that celebrates education also has to do with embracing the institutions that support it, namely, colleges and universities. It reflects a belief that endorsing learning establishments and attending them will mean that they in turn will support you back—that they will do right by you, help you, and lift you up.

Do people still feel this way?

They do not.

A 2011 Pew Research study shows that 57 percent of Americans think that higher education fails to provide good value.[2] A 2014 *Economist* article postulates that too many degrees are just wasted money.[3] And while a higher percentage of Americans are going to college than ever before, it probably doesn't help that the premium of having a four-year degree has actually flattened.[4] It now takes an additional degree at the graduate level to make more money. Just say the word "loans" to a few recent American college graduates and watch their reaction.

Now consider how the way we dress has changed in the last eight years.

Once upon a time, wearing a suit meant wanting to be taken seriously and aspiring to have others take you seriously.

The popularity of late Apple founder Steve Jobs's turtlenecks or Facebook chief Mark Zuckerberg's hooded sweatshirts indicates that perhaps that time has passed.[5]

Wearing a suit now might even have a deleterious effect in quite a few work circles; people might view the wearer as overdressed and think, *You're an idiot*, whereas the black turtleneck or hoody is considered serious: You're just too busy to think about being fancy. In fact, maybe you were too much of a genius to waste time going to classes. Didn't both Jobs and Zuckerberg drop out of college and become billionaires?

This countercultural shift in clothing rose as people started rebelling against institutions. In 2005 I did a story about how the Calvin Klein brand was funding this graffiti artist Claw Money. At the time it was a pretty crazy idea.[6] Graffiti was still illegal—after all, it was still midnight vandalism—but here it was being turned into something corporate? The notion really bothered people on both sides. It bothered graffiti artists who felt they were being asked to sell out. And it felt revolutionary to traditional apparel makers.

Fast forward to today. Now British street artist Banksy has licensed figurines for sale.[7]

What could be less illicit than that?

Tattoos have become common. The notion of suits versus rock and roll no longer exists. Everybody is weird, everybody has tatts, and everybody has nose piercings and is secretly riding motorcycles on the weekend or doing some odd, deviant art project.

Normalness is not valued the way it used to be. The mood at this moment could be considered very anti-1950s. Things have changed in the last decade; there is a current collective sentiment of *I don't give a damn*—that is, people enjoy the concept of being considered "weird." You can see that reflected in clothing that in recent years has popularized once-marginalized genres such as Comic-Con, which by 2015 grew to 167,000 attendees and multiple cities.[8] Perhaps nothing is more telling than the fact that McCall's, a clothing-pattern maker one might have once associated with 1950s housewives, is now selling cosplay costumes.[9] Subculture, meet Main Street.

The standard of disaffection and rejection of institutions is wildly reflected in Donald Trump's popularity. What is more of a proverbial middle finger at "institutions" than piercings? "Normcore" is considered a bad word.

#draintheswamp became the rallying and defining cry of Trump's voting bloc[10]—the wholesale rejection of the established. What applied in the populist uprising that garnered Trump his 62.9 million votes was a collective outcry to trash whatever was considered Establishment.[11]

Could we have read the graffiti licenses, tattoos, and piercings all the way to the polls? Can apparel forecast an election? Don't we have pollsters and countless tools that attempt to do this?

Consider the upset of the recent American election.[12]

The one that pollsters largely failed to predict.[13]

On August 29, 2005, a hurricane whipping to 174 miles per hour made landfall in Louisiana. Considered the United States' worst-ever natural disaster, Hurricane Katrina flooded over 90 percent of Mississippi beach towns and 80 percent of New Orleans, taking with it nearly two thousand lives across the seven states impacted and costing $108 billion in damage.[14]

What it also did was wipe out crocodile and ostrich farms in Florida and Louisiana.[15]

This was a small matter when compared to the lost lives and homes, and forever-eradicated memories and livelihoods. Twelve years later, New Orleans has not fully recovered. For obvious reasons, lost specialty farms were never going to get the attention or concern that other aspects of the storm's impact would. Does it truly matter if one can get an alligator bag when another person doesn't have a home in which to live?

Said small matter was the proverbial tree falling in a forest with no one to hear it, especially since it was falling in a forest during a raging wildfire. Yet there was something interesting about it.

Unlike other aspects of Katrina's lingering damage, this one can be seen by anyone in any retail store around the world. Before the hurricane, fashion largely divided into real furs and skins, and fairly obviously faux pelts and feathers. Snake and other skins, as well as ostrich and peacock feathers, are widely used in soft goods by everyone from Armani to Chanel. After the storm the Louisiana Department of Wildlife and Fisheries noted that hurricanes such as Katrina and Rita would affect availability of these materials.[16]

Katrina damaged more than $90 million in protected wildlife alone. It was estimated that sea turtle nests along the Alabama coast and at Bon Secour National Wildlife Refuge were destroyed; trees fell at Noxubee National Wildlife, including all the ones that housed endangered red-cockaded woodpeckers; and approximately half of the Breton National Wildlife Refuge was washed away. What couldn't be completely measured was the impact to unprotected species, such as crocodiles and alligators, and to pelt-producing farms.

This wasn't unprecedented. Previous nature events have impacted soft goods. Bird flu has led to feather shortages. Designer Donald Pliner once mentioned that leather prices had spiked 10 to 20 percent during the mad cow disease outbreak.[17]

But fashion responded in a surprisingly expedient way; it improved its imitation wares. If Hurricane Katrina had not happened, faux fur would still be cheap and tacky, resembling a bad Halloween boa. Overnight, fake skins and fake furs dramatically improved.[18]

Who knew that the technology was there all along?

How much of an improvement was there? So much that in December 2007, the Royal Society for the Prevention of Cruelty to Animals indicated that real rabbit and fox fur was being peddled at TK Maxx, a British discount retailer, as the synthetics acrylic, polyester, and nylon.[19] More recent spot checks by British tabloid *The Sun* and the free daily paper *Metro* indicate that today's goods make it a challenge for some to distinguish between some real and fake furs.[20]

Nowhere remotely near Louisiana. In fact, 4,625 miles away, to be precise.[21]

And more than ten years later.

In other words, the long-lasting effects of the world's nature-driven disasters and the planet's rapidly shifting environment will now be seen and felt forever—and by anyone—just by going into a clothing retailer, even a niche one, anywhere in the world.

It is easy for us to dismiss fashion as something trivial.

To many, "fashion" is embodied by Meryl Streep's notorious editor in the movie *The Devil Wears Prada*, who infamously declared that Anne Hathaway's character had not chosen the blue color of her sweater, but the fashion elite in some rarefied office had chosen it for her.

To be honest, that kind of fashion is only interesting to a niche audience. This book is not about that room or even whether blue is this season's shade. Rather, it will address how that sweater reflects larger world concerns and how wearing it can shape the future.

Because this is not a book about fashion. That is, it is not a book about dress hemlines so much as it is about cultural trendlines such as the stories above. Does subculture clothing signify a political shift rising to the top?

Can we see the lasting effects of natural disasters in retailers nowhere near the disaster site?

What is really happening in the world around us?

Going one step further, can clothing be the canary in a coal mine that shows us what needs improving in our world?

This is a book not about polka dots and color trends, but about what you can learn by observing movements, such as the above, in the $300 billion soft-goods industry.

This book is about how things you see every day present a way to take the pulse of the population at large, and understand where the world is at and where it's going. You can use clothing, as I have, to read the cultural zeitgeist, predict world changes, make more money, see the next big world occurrence, and possibly learn about ways you may save your own life.

I will make three main points about clothing and our world:

1. Clothing tells you what large groups of people are thinking, better than they can tell you themselves.
2. Clothing can tell you about big world events, providing an early barometer of how people are reacting to—or about to react to—economics, culture, world events, and natural disasters.

3. Clothing is capable of impacting world events. It can shape the future. More importantly, we can use it to alter our outcome.

We will explore the link between bankers' superstitious clothing and recessions . . . how clothing is a financial weapon in a divorce . . . why choosing the wrong textile could cause famine in Africa . . . which popular breakfast food is a new conflict diamond . . . how a shoe could power a city grid . . . if wearing a watch could save your life in an earthquake.

At the end of some pop econ books, authors will suggest that their books have not materially changed your world, or that the aspects you've read might not be harnessed to change the world around you. I am going to do the opposite. The purpose of this book is to get you thinking about a tool that is right at your fingertips. It is quite literally woven into your very existence.

Let us begin.

ARE YOU WEARING YOUR LUCKY JERSEY?

PEOPLE LIKE to believe they are logical and that the world runs on measured judgments—facts. So why is it that in times of crisis we turn to superstition?

In 2007, when things were good in the financial markets, I wrote an article about bankers and their lucky boxer shorts. At the time, I was writing about style for the *Financial Times*. But I wasn't really writing about style, at least not in terms of whether designers were showing higher or lower hemlines. Rather, I was tracking how clothing was reflective of the world we lived in. Or I was reading cues of what was yet to come. More on this later.

I was at the opening of the Hermès on Wall Street, where Dom Perignon champagne and top-shelf Macallan Scotch poured so freely that bankers told me, well, pretty much anything: questionable stock tips, stories about misadventures at Scores strip club, but also which Hermès items were their lucky charms and what they wore to the office to stack the odds of the day in their favor.

The most memorable visual was how many traders would only trade if they had on their rally cap, a baseball hat worn by traders to go with the "rally monkey," a YouTube clip of a monkey dancing to the '90s House of Pain song, "Jump Around."

It transpired that when times were tough, bankers relied on superstition. Just about every banker has some quirk, Charles Nelson at the Baron Group merchant bank told me.[1] At Fortunoff jewelers, traders were known to buy two pairs of the bear-and-bull cuff links and immediately throw out the bears before even leaving the store. A bull economy is, after all, positive, whereas its opposite, a bear market, refers to hibernating bears, a negative economic situation. It turns out that many bankers don't just have rally caps—they have lucky suits, lucky boxers, lucky jewelry, and lucky socks. One told me that if his lucky suit was at the dry cleaners, he didn't even go to the office.

The Hermès party was one of two over-the-top megaparties to happen in the financial district that year. The other was Tiffany & Co., whose shindig was so ridiculously lavish that it featured individual blue, box-shaped cakes with little ribbons and gifts of limited edition key chains for the hundreds of attendees. Tiffany giving away its goods like candy? This should have meant the good times were just that—so good.

While I kept my observations in *Financial Times* to just an article about lucky charms, I was noticing something more. The parties should have been nothing but mirth, but bankers at both seemed particularly anxious, as though there was something brewing under all that single malt and exuberance.

At the Tiffany & Co. event, I overheard would-be shoppers ask each other about popular items that other bankers had bought. Why, in fact, were they buying so many lucky cuff links? And if luck was on their minds, what were they really "telling" me?

It seems they felt overwhelmed with a need to stack the odds in their favor. Earl Thorpe Jr., at the time a sales trader for Jefferies, indicated that a colleague he knew at one of the major banks had taken to forbidding staff from wearing the "unlucky" color yellow.[2]

That bank turned out to be the ill-fated Lehman Brothers.

There was something in the undercurrent—or in this case, the underpinnings—of what people were wearing that foreshadowed something that hadn't even happened yet.

Another ex-trader, Cormac Glynn, who was running the Wall Street Wonders consultancy, confirmed the mood. "You're either a total success or a total failure. So in the same way you never walk under a ladder or to avoid hiccups you crawl under a donkey, wearing red means you're bullish about the market. It's an all-or-nothing game."[3]

But while one could make a case that one person was superstitious or possibly one department was suffering, the heightened focus on luck, and indeed chance and destiny, was playing out in front of my eyes, and not just with one superstitious person. I spoke to traders and investment bankers from no fewer than twenty companies.

In journalism, we have a saying: One occurrence is an isolated incident, two is a coincidence, three is a trend. Criminologists and forensic investigators even go so far as to believe that there is no such thing as coincidence, that two incidents are worth examining. I was seeing many more than two or three.

Mark LaFlamme, an Asian-markets trader, told of a colleague who embodied homeless chic. "The first time I saw him at ABN-AMRO, I thought he was a half-senile underpaid back office worker, waiting for retirement." The colleague sported a shirt with elbows worn-through and pants whose pockets were coming off. And in fact, had suddenly taken to wearing the same shirt and trousers every day for two straight weeks.[4]

Turns out that the coworker's outfit had been one he had originally worn once during better days. When he had been having a good streak.

I thought of this story again during the market turmoil.

Now, of course, we look back on the economy and we know what transpired, Lehman Brothers collapsed and started a tidal wave that led to an economic tsunami around the world.[5]

But back then, even though the larger public may not have been aware, each morning started an already worrisome day for the finance industry. No one knew what the day would bring. And therefore bankers, at the heart of everyone's concerns, were focused on stacking the odds in their favor. The markets were rolling, and each day presented new fears.

In reality, many of us believe in luck and are superstitious. How many times have you heard the phrase, "Knock on wood"? You may not even think twice about saying it. Consider the phrase, "Everything happens for a reason," often deployed when we have no rational explanation for occurrences. Or how about that old goodie, "It's part of God's plan." The act of applying authorship or intentionality in the world when things may seem random is called *teleogical reasoning*.[6] We employ it when things occur that feel senseless, when no amount of logic makes sense of an event. It allows us to cope and stay sane in the face of situations that may seem purposeless. Invoking destiny is part of the human condition. Luck and the notion of chance are widespread.

Common superstitions include not walking under ladders or not wanting to see a bride in her wedding dress before the ceremony. Italians fear the number *seventeen*: If you invite people to dinner and seventeen people RSVP, you either have to disinvite someone or invite one more person. The Chinese don't favor living in homes with the number four in the address or having a four in one's phone number, as the homonym for four is, ominously "death." And why bring death any closer than it already is?

But bankers participate in one of the most analysis-based economies. Wall Street has more analysts and macros and charts than most university math departments. On average, Goldman Sachs hires 90 to 120 new analysts every year.[7] The financial modeling industry, that is, the abstract analysis of what will occur in a real-world financial situation, is a multimillion-dollar business. [8] After all, billions of dollars depend on it. It includes option pricing, derivatives (and all its variations, credit derivatives, exotic derivatives), credit scoring, risk modeling, real options, and so forth.[9] Luck or chance is the very opposite of this decision tree.

And superstition is pejorative. It is linked with guessing and the supernatural. The *Oxford English Dictionary* would say it has to do with "old wives' tale," "myth," "fallacy," or even worse, "delusion." Bankers are the opposite of whom we would expect, and hope, would rely on superstition.

So why are so many bankers superstitious?

One reason may be that superstition is linked to control.

A 2010 Kansas State Study showed that people utilize superstition in order to feel or gain control over their lives and uncertainty.[10] The same Kansas State University study showed that superstitious behavior included actions such as wearing a lucky jersey or lucky charms.

Superstition is not even solely a human condition. In 1947, B. F. Skinner, a psychiatrist who had long analyzed the notion of free will and operant condition, showed that pigeons could be trained to become superstitious. He rewarded unusual and illogical behaviors, linking them to positive rewards. In other words, when the birds connected certain illogical actions to positive results, they repeated the peculiar actions in an attempt to re-create the benefits.[11] Ergo, lots of creatures can be trained to repeat nonsensical actions if there is a slight chance, much less full promise, of favorable outcomes.

If, therefore, a banker had worn a rally cap on a day when things went well, then it stood to reason that he or she might wear it again. And if the ensuing day went poorly, it could certainly be blamed on other things, but would one chance not wearing the cap?

What is the harm after all in "knocking on wood"? None. So why wouldn't you? And just imagine what might happen if you didn't.

But did buying all those charms reflect another kind of fear? A subconscious fear that the house of cards was all about to come down?

In 2009 we saw another spike in the purchase of charms. It was the year fashion saw rising sales of the hamsa, the Turkish hand symbol linked to warding off evil.[12]

This time it was around fears that the world would actually—not just economically—end. After all, we were nearing 2012, the year Nostradamus had predicted our global demise. Obviously, the world did not end that December, but we thought it would.

A quick Google search at the end of 2009 indicated a staggering 233 million results that described the phenomenon and linked to at least thirty websites dedicated to obsessing about whether the end of the world was coming. (In fact, those sites still exist, only now with various quirky explanations for our date miscalculations, of course.) The most prominent site included one at History.com called "Nostradamus: 2012," another a numerology site, and a third entitled The End, which connected the end of times to economic crisis.

At least eighteen documentaries were produced and aired on the topic. And as though certifying a true pop phenomenon, Hollywood delivered two major motion pictures: the movie *2012*, from Roland Emmerich and Paramount Pictures, starring John Cusack and Danny Glover, followed by *2012: The War for Souls*, a Michael Bay flick from Whitley Strieber's book of the same name. There was even an economics-themed movie, *Death Race* (the new release, not the classic), which referenced 2012 as the year that the economy finally fails altogether. That Harold Camping predicted (incorrectly) that the world would end did not stop the fears.

Whether logical or not, we feared and still fear the end of the world. And we wore those superstitions. The soft-goods and accessories industries saw increased sales in amulets and charms. Evil-eye symbology made it to the collections of numerous jewelry designer collections.

The influential British department store Liberty reported a spike in talisman jewelry. Designers who heavily featured luck-themed sayings and symbols—for example, Alex and Ani or Me & Ro—saw booms in their collections.[13]

Part of the reason for our use of lucky items may be that we believe they work.

In a study at the University of Cologne, psychologist Lysann Damisch found that participants who were handed "lucky" golf balls landed 35 percent more golf putts than those who were told their balls were regular. The belief that one had luck on one's side actually created better performance.[14]

Another form of putting our hands into chance is, of course, prayer. In 2015, Duke University's Harold G. Koenig, MD, director of Duke's Center for Spirituality, Theology and Health, conducted an analysis of more than 1,500 reputable medical studies and came to the conclusion that "people who are more religious and pray more have better mental and physical health."[15]

In the 1870s Francis Galton was the first to attempt to summarize whether prayer would have an effect. He analyzed with humor that, given how often the British royal family's longevity was prayed for, its members should live nearly forever.[16] Of course the efficacy of prayer has been much argued and debated. In 2006, the well-known STEP project by Harvard professor Herbert Benson studied 1,802 coronary-artery-bypass patients and came to the conclusion that, in fact, those who received prayer fared neither better nor worse, but those who were told they would receive prayer suffered complications and mortality because they believed they were so ill as to need it.[17] That is, it is not whether prayer works or doesn't work; it is that people believe there is a reason for prayer and that prayer has an effect—just as we believe a lucky shirt or a lucky golf ball will work better for us.

Crosses have always sold well. But beginning in 2008, suddenly they were doing even better. Religious symbols, crosses, Jewish stars, and other elements linked to spirituality, were all popular. The legendary costume jeweler Kenneth J. Lane reported that between the years 2008 and 2012 he suddenly saw an enormous spike in demand for his crosses, not only for the existing designs but showed me a wall of crosses, which featured twice as many new designs. Lane's business is well established and has been steady for many decades; he famously dressed Jackie Onassis and Elizabeth Taylor.[18] Given the volume the company does and that he has largely sold the same popular styles for many decades, a noticeable spike from KJL meant much more than just some claim of company growth.[19]

If some charms are designed to stack the odds in our favor, then others we worry will sway things toward poor outcomes. Just as bankers throw out the bear half of the cuff links, no one wants to be carrying around something that might tip the scales against us.

We routinely engage in behaviors to knock away bad luck and we believe that the act of doing so is effective in pushing away potential harmful effects.[20]

In August 2006, I had the misfortune of being on assignment away from home when the London terrorist plot was foiled. That was the incident where twenty-four suspects were charged with plotting to detonate liquid explosives on seven flights traveling between the United Kingdom, the United States, and Canada. In order to be allowed to fly home to New York, I FedEx'd all my luggage home and went to the airport carrying only my passport. No cell phone. No book. Empty-handed. I'd forgotten about just one small thing.

Earlier that week, I had been at a market appointment, the fashion equivalent of a meet-and-greet, at Garrard, the jewelry company. In their Albemarle Street store, the creative director, Jade Jagger, had installed a gigantic gumball machine from which one could get a piece of Garrard jewelry, dispensed like a candied bauble.

My spin yielded a sterling silver gun charm, a tiny thing of about one eighth of an inch in length on a chain necklace, befitting of Jagger's rock-and-roll roots. I put on the trinket. And forgot about it.

Until I reached security at London Stansted.

The security agent who stopped me said, "You're wearing a gun." I replied, "It's not a gun; it's a pendant? It's obviously not real."

"It doesn't matter that it's not a real gun; it's what it represents. You can't travel with it." I was gobsmacked. The necklace came off, or I wasn't traveling.

Subsequently I wrote about the experience, and in doing so, I interviewed Franco Pianegonda and Loree Rodkin, two different jewelry designers known for their spikes and danger symbols. Travelers were reporting that all over the world TSA agents were calling into question the symbols in their clothing—and having the travelers remove them.[21]

The actions didn't need to be rational. The TSA knew my charm couldn't actually cause harm. However, it did not matter.

If you have ever been in a knockdown, drag-out fight with a significant other, you may recall a time when you came to the table with ironclad logic, facts, and rational thinking on your side. You thought for sure, when presented with logic, your significant other would see "reason." Were you surprised when he or she simply didn't see things your way?

But fact-based decision-making is not all that is behind the choices we make. In some instances, fact may not even be the prevailing factor. In 2009 brain researcher Antonio Damasio theorized that we base many of our decisions on emotion.[22]

In other words, my gun charm and the spikes worn by other people may symbolize intent. Or they may not. But they caused fear.

And our fears are reflected early in these gestures, carrying charms or amulets. I may not be around to see you pray or tee off that lucky golf ball, but I can see with my eyes if you're wearing a hamsa. I can see if you're wearing a gun symbol, which might indicate an affinity for violence. And it supersedes any logic when it comes to dealing with the unknown, the end of the world, or terrorism.

We wear our emotions, and possibly our intent.

In July 2015, Bremen Airport in Germany banned a gun-themed bag created by the Dutch design group Vlieger and Vandam.[23] The purse, which features the outline of a pistol heat-pressed into the leather implies that the carrier is literally carrying. Popular with celebrities such as singers Rihanna and Rita Ora and *Sports Illustrated* model Irina Shayk, one could argue that a gun would not cause such a prominent and immovable outline in leather. Going one step further, the expensive item was largely being carried by famous cover girls. Are supermodels packing heat when they go to restaurants? Probably not; nonetheless, even knockoffs of the bag have been pulled from shelves in New York.[24]

Our emotions are reflected early in fashion. Before the financial crisis (and well before it hit the news), there was a spike in bankers wearing lucky tokens. And right after the bomb scare, you couldn't go anywhere wearing anything that symbolized danger without people looking at you like you were a terrorist.

And as far back as 2008, jewelers started making "end of the world" amulets that purported to save you. From peperoncinos to the Eye of Horus to the Atlantean Symbol to the Oracle of Delphi, jewelry lines claimed to protect you from everything from swine flu to the cataclysmic

2012. Jewelry probably isn't going to save you from the end of the world, but yet amulets have sold like hotcakes. What should we read into it when we see that there is an increasing trend in the reliance on superstition?

Whether it's an impending global crash or a reaction to either ecological disaster or terrorism, the age-old response of hiding behind familiar symbols lives on. We each seek flags of recognition, reject anything different, and use overt symbolism to appear to be one of the crowd and gain comfort from it.

Consider the messaging of Lance Armstrong's once-popular Livestrong bracelet. The bracelets, which went on to spawn a million rubber facsimiles for various causes, were not a fashion statement. They were technically apparel, as they were worn. However, they were about the message—the message of belonging.

Similarly, those who follow the kabbalah faith wear red-string bracelets on their left wrists, to communicate to others their clanship. "I am one of you," the bracelet says. "I share the same values." In American student societies, sororities and fraternities have symbols, such as a sheaf of wheat for Alpha Omicron Pi, which designates the wearer as part of the club.

I know something about you, and you know something about me, even though we are strangers who've just met, the symbol says. We are part of the same crowd. The worn symbols provide messaging, and that messaging provides recognition and, in turn, comfort.

Clothing tells you about what is on the minds of others: what worries them, what they are thinking about, what they hope for, what they fear. The messaging can be so strong as to be a problem unto itself. In 2011, a woman in New York was actually arrested for wearing a ring shaped as a small rocket and, ironically, carrying the message, "War Is Over." Although the traveler offered to throw away the antiwar costume jewelry, she was still detained and ultimately charged for simply possessing the ring.[25] Her ring spoke for her so loudly—she theorized that it may have been perceived as slightly bullet-shaped—that her actual voice was drowned in the message. Her intent, lost.

While such stories are great water-cooler fodder—"Did you hear about the woman who got arrested . . . for wearing a ring!"—they also are front-row observations. Observations to which you have access.

In 1943 the psychologist Abraham Maslow created a pyramid of needs, a hierarchical chart outlining what we as human beings seek out.

He theorized that at our primary level, physiology, we require and care about only three things to sustain our basic selves: food/water, shelter, and clothing. Everything else is a bonus.

These are the big three that everyone seeks. Everyone experiences them. Everyone is exposed to great volumes of them on a daily and consistent basis. They will form the basis of what you think is most important in your everyday life.

Food, housing, and clothing.

You won't necessarily ever see where I live, nor will you see the homes of the majority of your colleagues and acquaintances. The same goes for food. You won't be with most of the people you interact with at the majority of their meals. Instagram photos don't count.

You will, however, see clothing.

And clothing is talking to you.

One group that knows this are psychics. Whether or not you believe in the power of extrasensory perception, in recent years wannabe psychics have been dismantled as frauds for using a technique called "cold reading." Cold reading is a magician's trick; it homes in on topics every person cares about, such as relationships and money. Universal concerns about love and loss. In cold readings, a would-be psychic uses subtle clues and feedback to go through a series of statements about you, which may or may not be correct. That person counts on you to remember the correct statements and forget the missed hits. "Wow, I *am* worried about my family," you might say.

One powerful tool in the cold-reading process is what you are wearing. Even more importantly, the jewelry you are wearing, particularly any religious or symbolic pieces.[26]

In this instance, it is not important whether or not you believe in psychics; what is important is that those who purport to have the gift have homed in on the messaging of your clothing. They know that your apparel speaks volumes. Without you ever saying a word.

I have an old joke from all the economics and statistics I studied: "87 percent of all statistics are made up on the spot." What this refers to is how many of the studies available to us make use of manipulated data. Consider, for example, the study funded by a pharmaceutical company that might have selected subjects already predisposed to favor certain outcomes. Or more egregiously, the study that is presented to you as ironclad fait accompli, when it may have only measured the thoughts or reactions of, say, ten people. Ten would not be the number a scientist would deem statistically relevant, that is, an adequate sample size to make that study something from which you can extrapolate information about the general population.

A random tidbit for you: When you hear that x number of people watched the Super Bowl this year, it isn't because your local bar (and every cable company) took a head count. That number is derived from Nielsen NetRatings set-top boxes. Approximately fifteen thousand set-top boxes sit in television homes across the United States.[27] Those households have been selected to represent, well, everyone. What percentage of those boxes are tuned to the Super Bowl is then extrapolated, multiplied by an exponential of how many people live in the United States.

Whether any of those fifteen thousand people adequately represent you personally? Well, that's much debated. However, the takeaway is that this is similar to how medical studies are done. The best ones have large sample sizes. Simply put, the greater the sample size in data collection, the greater the confidence interval or the less room for error.

While these anecdotes about charms may seem like anecdotes, they are not just that. They are dozens if not hundreds of points of data. You are collecting them without even knowing it, and you are collecting lots of them. Every day. In essence, you are your own marketing study.

Each day you will likely encounter dozens if not thousands of points of clothing. Unless you work from home alone and you choose not to open the door to even your mail carrier, that number is upwards of one. If you live in New York City and you take the subway, that number is in the hundreds; 5.7 million people ride the subway every day.[28] If you are a celebrity, one event alone could expose you to ten thousand points of clothing.

Funders and Founders, a group that analyzed the effect of an entrepreneur's product impact, estimates that in an average year, you will interact with eighty thousand people, including three new people every single day. That's interaction, not just visual observation.[29]

Those interactions can involve dozens of levels of influence, according to sociologist Max Weber, who analyzed many levels of social contact.[30]

In Claude S. Fischer's *To Dwell among Friends: Personal Networks in Town and City*, the nature of your influence is even more highly impactful. As many as 167 people a day care about your actions, small or large.[31]

Without knowing it, you are also storing that information. You pass by a person on the street, and subconsciously your brain records what you have seen. Human memory varies. In a retention interval of one week, some people will retain as much as 98 percent, some as low as 11 percent. But researcher Will Thalheimer's study on forgetfulness[32] concluded that on average you may remember as much as 23 percent of the details you saw at a given time, even after a whole week.

If you have hyperthymesia or HSAM (highly superior autobiographical memory), you even remember every single detail of every day for years.

What this amounts to is that you see, and note, dozens of details about clothing on a daily basis. To reiterate, this is not about style or fashion; it is about a simple touchpoint that you encounter constantly.

Sum up the week and then the month, and now you are looking at thousands of tiny messages. Of hopes, of fear, of worry.

Right before the financial crisis, I had breakfast with Martha Stewart. The home tycoon mentioned to me that sales of home goods were through the roof. People were nesting, looking for comfort. And it wasn't just home goods. It was clothing too: ponchos, blanket coats, woven items from the home that could be worn outdoors.

Around this time, designers started to make clothing that I coined as "old man chic." Designers more commonly known for sexy red carpet clothing such Roberto Cavalli reported a brisk business in cardigans more suitable to geriatric homebodies. Opticians such as Luxottica and Robert Marc indicated to me that people were buying tortoiseshell glasses that made them look older, and wearing them without prescriptions. Bifocals, without the focal. Savile Row tailors breathed a sigh of relief; tweed was back. Psychoanalyst Robert Schwalbe, the author of *Sixty, Sexy, and Successful*, told me, "With too much changing in the economic environment, the young man who dresses in the classics of rounded glasses, cuffed trousers, bow ties, and elbow patches is turning to a look of assurance and continuance."[33]

Clothing is a way to take an early measure of what large groups of people are thinking. Each person alone is an anecdote. Hundreds or thousands of touchpoints is a pattern. By paying attention to these symbols—especially when they defy logic and reason—and trying to discern whether they emerge outside of rational thinking in any consistent way, you can use clothing (and jewelry) to see early—and often before everyone else—how people are coping with crisis. When symbols are superseding the rational, and bankers are relying on superstition over math, pay attention.

But know that you are already absorbing the information.

Your brain stores information in several ways. There's *declarative memory*: facts such as your birthday. *Episodic memory*: an event, such as your first day of work. *Procedural memory*: the ability to write your name or drive a car. *Semantic memory*: concepts you've learned, such as what you are learning here. *Spatial memory*: a map of your surroundings. You are already noting the elements I am talking about. They belong in a category of brain function called "working memory." This is where the brain absorbs fractions of information, until you decide whether to keep the detail. The good news is that you are already seeing these patterns, every day; you simply have to connect them, as I have. The brain stores memory trace, the initial element in a neuronic ensemble.[34] When you go on to retell yourself a story, then it becomes a long-term memory. All you need to do to take memory trace out of storage is to start to pay attention.

Try this: For one week, starting from when you put down this chapter, make a note of how many times you see red neckties. Or you can pick another touchpoint: Rolex watches or blue-striped button-down shirts or tortoise-shell eyeglasses; anything will do. Just choose something specific.

Make a conscious note of what you're seeing and just start counting. At the end of the week, how many items did you see?

The purpose of this exercise is for you to do something that I have been doing innately every day for twenty years. Later, I'll help you to hone what you're choosing to count. But for now, just start counting. I simply want you to go from unconscious to conscious in how visuals register with you.

There's a benefit to spotting these patterns. You might simply want to know more about the people around you and what's on their minds. You may simply want to channel your inner psychic at your next cocktail party. Perhaps you want to know the mood of your colleagues or company. Is your boss nervous these days? Maybe you want to know how your significant other is feeling. What are your neighbors thinking?

But you may even be able to take advantage of the financial opportunity in situations. Consider companies that acted on early indicators of nervousness or fear. As people became concerned about the end of the world, the California company Vivos started marketing and building an underground shelter in Kansas for the five thousand people who, after the apocalypse, would then run the rest of the planet.[35] Demand in Kansas halted somewhat, so the company has upped the ante with a shelter intended for six thousand, in Rothenstein, Germany, just in case. They say it will feature a zoo, swimming pools, theaters, gyms, restaurants, and custom apartments, able to withstand nuclear blast, chemical agents, earthquakes, tsunamis, or some such other disasters. Speculations are that the property is worth $1.1 billion.[36]

In fact, there are some companies that accurately predicted Hurricane Sandy. They invested in disaster-recovery firms and generators. Currently temporary generators are sold out across the United States, and companies selling gas-powered, permanent generators are booked six months out. With the additional multibillion-dollar effort slated for recovery, certain parties will benefit. What would have happened if you'd spotted it coming?

Large groups of people are telling you what they're thinking. You have a way of knowing without them saying it.

Clothing can speak volumes.

You just have to listen.

YOU ALREADY KNOW IF THAT'S A FAKE IN THE MUSEUM

Brian: I am *not* the Messiah!
Arthur: I say you are, Lord, and I should know. I've followed a few.

—from *Monty Python's Life of Brian*

I N THE LAST chapter, we saw how clothing reflects our rational or irrational beliefs, and how paying attention to what people are wearing can alert us to changes in the world around us.

Bankers show us that we are wearing our worries on our sleeves—literally. And you saw how people's reactions to weaponized jewelry or dangerous clothing symbols can alert you to how deeply concerned large groups of people are about terrorism, including in ways that are often not consciously acknowledged.

If you tried the exercise of counting, say, baseball hats or team jerseys, you have started to harness your ability to measure the indications of those fears. By the end of this book, you will see that even simply flipping through the racks at certain stores can alert you to a possible economic rise or fall. But I'm getting ahead of myself.

In the book *Getting to Yes*,[1] Roger Fisher and William Ury talk extensively about the importance of listening well when it comes to negotiations or sales. They refer to "perception," putting yourself in another party's shoes, "emotion," recognizing and understanding the emotions of the person you're trying to convince or sell to, and of course, "communication," or listening actively and acknowledging what is being said by another person. Being better attuned to others will help you.

This book is about how to do just that by using a tool (actually, countless tools) that are right in front of you.

In this chapter, I'll talk about a con that is going on as we speak. You'll see how that con, one that may seem to start esoterically, with clothing, turns up in lots of other areas of our lives through other cons—small and large—and we'll see how clothing provides front-row evidence to the pervasive behaviors that are at the root of all those illusions.

Let's start with a hypothetical: You save up all your life for a trip to Paris. Perhaps this is what your spouse wants for your tenth anniversary. You go online, you rent a cute pied-à-terre overlooking the Eiffel Tower, and when you land, you make the requisite visits to Notre-Dame and Sacré-Coeur. Then you wend your way toward the Louvre, through the beautiful swings of the Tuileries Gardens. In the most romantic moment of the trip, you stand hugging shoulder-to-shoulder in the hallowed hallways of the Louvre, looking at the *Mona Lisa*'s cryptic smile.

Which is a fake.

Stop. This isn't *The Da Vinci Code*. It's a hypothetical.

But, really, how do we know when we see something in the museum that we are looking at the real deal? We believe we know because someone has told us it is so. We believe that when we walk through the hallways of the Louvre or the Metropolitan Museum of Art in New York, or the Guggenheim in Bilbao—wherever we may be—that what is on the walls and in the hallways is bona fide. That is, the *Mona Lisa* has been verified by experts we trust. We may not know those experts ourselves, but we believe when we walk into the museum that *someone* who is accountable would not have put a piece into a collection or on display without the item having gone through an extensive verification process.

However, a conspiracy to show you fakes in the museums is underway. Shocked? Let me tell you how this all came to be.

Every September, magazine editors, models, fashion designers, advertising sales folks, celebrities, and a hodgepodge of other types gather the week after Labor Day for New York Fashion Week, a two-week[2] extravaganza of runway shows where designers preview the next season's clothes.

During the autumn of 2008, at one of the most anticipated Fashion Week cocktail parties, revelers such as model Agyness Deyn, photographer Ellen Von Unwerth, art scion Chiara Clemente, and designer Yigal Azrouel packed into Christie's auction house to get first glimpses of some 229 fashion items in transit to London for an October 30 sale.

Clothing, jewelry, and headwear from designers such as Andre Courreges, Ossie Clark, Azzedine Alaia, Gianni Versace, Issey Miyake, Paco Rabanne, and Malcolm McLaren/Vivienne Westwood held the rapt attention of partygoers whose normal focus at fashion parties might be catching up with each other after a summer apart. This wasn't surprising, as preauction buzz had it that some pieces might fetch as much as fifteen thousand dollars.[3]

Particularly eye-catching, though, were two shirts labeled to be from Vivienne Westwood and Malcolm McLaren's late-1970s "Seditionaries" collection.

To the crowd, the shirts seemed, well, wearable, especially when compared to a Paco Rabanne bird-cage gown made entirely of silver links, or a fitted cutout Thierry Mugler gown just like the one worn by Demi Moore in *Indecent Proposal*. After all, only a collector spends tens of thousands on an item that hangs in the closet, but for the partygoers—of which a good chunk were good-looking, straight men—a thousand or two for a piece of punk culture they could actually wear? In their size? Now that was interesting.

And it instantly set this auction apart from any other art sale in one key regard: Everyone bidding was a qualified appraiser. Shirts don't require the trained eye one would need to recognize Da Vinci.

The sale represented the entire private collection of shop owners Mark Haddawy and Katy Rodriguez, owners of a vintage store.[4]

But there was a problem with this sale—one big problem.

Malcolm McLaren claimed the McLaren/Westwood items were fakes.[5] McLaren, the longtime rabble-rouser, punk-band founder, designer, and former romantic partner to Vivienne Westwood, alleged that Christie's, Haddawy, and Rodriguez knew that the pieces in the sale weren't authentic, were deliberately ignoring him, and were intentionally swindling the unsuspecting buyer and general public[6]—you.

McLaren had, as it turns out, been waging a multidecade, multicontinent campaign against sales of the clothing he and Vivienne Westwood had made together.[7] His efforts had involved museums; auction houses across the world; British, American, and Japanese customs officials; other government officials; celebrities; art authorities; book publishers—a long laundry list of names. The week prior to my interview with him, he had been working with Scotland Yard, which had raided a warehouse of Westwood/McLaren fakes in Croydon. Partygoers—in particular, the actual potential bidders for the clothes—were likely to have heard something about these events, the latest in McLaren's long history of public and controversial battles.

In 1972 McLaren and Westwood had opened the Let It Rock store on London's King's Road, selling 1950s clothes and memorabilia.[8]

Nowadays, the King's Road is littered with apparel chain shops, dominated by British names such as Accessorize, Office shoes, and Whistles, alongside the other retail "musts" of any large British shopping street—an Orange telecom retail store, a Boots drugstore, and so forth. Will anything being sold there today end up in any museum? Probably not. Even the Saatchi Gallery and the farmers market (selling its outlandishly priced blocks of Colston Bassett Stilton) have a slightly corporate air to them.

But this was not the look of the King's Road in the early '70s, when the street was decidedly rougher. Instead of yummy mummies with strollers, thrift stores and disenfranchised youth populated the corners. This was the crowd that came to McLaren and Westwood's shop. Within two years in this environment, McLaren, who had heard the band the New York Dolls, had decided that style of music was the next big thing, renamed their shop SEX, started peddling punk rock paraphernalia and apparel, and went searching for a band he could push on to fame.[9]

In 1975 he cobbled together his dream band, the Sex Pistols, and arranged to manage them. By 1976 the band, who couldn't stay in tune or sing much, were signed to the record label EMI.

As they often showed up drunk, liked to curse on stage, verbally abused reporters, and feuded among themselves in between drug-hazed binges, it was almost inevitable they would disband a mere two years later. But in the brief period between creation and dissolution, they immortalized punk culture as we know it today.

Now, all the details of McLaren and the Sex Pistols' fascinating lives aside, what I want you to remember, is this:

It was a massively influential period in recent cultural history.

It was a very short period in time.

During this period, McLaren and Westwood hit on something they could not have predicted would endure: the punk look. Their store became a hangout for the punk types, and together the two designed several influential clothing collections that became the subject of many books, auctions, and museum collections—the cornerstone of this story. From the images of youth in skintight clothes to certain sounds in today's music, to clothes we purchase (this includes anything with a safety pin or image of a skull, mind you), those two to three years continue to epitomize cool, inspiring, and generating art, culture, and product.[10]

After the Sex Pistols, McLaren tried to leave those years behind. He did lots of other things, including restyling Adam and the Ants, forming Bow Wow Wow, releasing *The Great Rock'n'Roll Swindle*. When he and Westwood parted ways, he even went on to Hollywood, dated model Lauren Hutton, and worked with movie director Steven Spielberg. But ultimately punk and its legacy defined his life and came back to haunt McLaren for the better part of two decades, all the way up to his death in April 2010.

Let's get back to the auction in 2008.

A key part of the Christie's sale, thirty-two lots, or items, were said to be from Westwood and McLaren's King's Road boutique, drawn from three collections, "Let It Rock," "Sex," and "Seditionaries." At auction, these garments have always commanded top price in any sale. They are seen as more than clothing, as significant artifacts sought after by museums and collectors alike for their visual representation of the punk movement.

The fact that in addition to making the clothes, the duo clothed many of the '60s and '70s punk icons (including New York Dolls guitarist Sylvain Sylvain and of course Sid Vicious) made the objects worth more. Two items from the auction included pieces designed for Sly Stone (of Sly and the Family Stone), including a studded black-leather jacket worn on the cover of Stone's 1973 album *Fresh*.

McLaren was sure the garments at the auction house were knockoffs. He told me on October 1, 2008,[11] "Of course they're not genuine! I wrote Christie's a complicated letter explaining why, and they said they would look into it but they didn't. It's not necessarily a cottage industry, but most things were made in a 'kitchen table way,' mostly by hand. As an artist, which I am and what I was trained at for eight years, you recognize what you've made by your own hand! I never used Stalin in the Anarchists prints, or I look for when the handwriting is not my own. I saw things I personally have never designed nor made, inside the Christie's preview. They had two T-shirts with Little Richard, one in black and one in white, both enormous, for giants. We only made things in one size and that size was 'Vivienne.' I would fit the clothes on her. The people we were selling to were ages fourteen, fifteen, sixteen, and scrawny. People back then, if they'd had too many hamburgers, the sweat would be pouring off their brow trying to get into them! At the preview, I saw two very large shirts, almost the size of portly middle-aged men! I could get two people of that era into them! Any fool could tell from a distance!"

He went on to point out another obvious discrepancy: "How do [they possibly] think all these clothes survived thirty years? These clothes were never made in enormous quantities. Of the Anarchy shirt we didn't make more than forty, maximum fifty. And you have to think they were fifty pounds in 1970 and it was a lot of money then, so these kids saved and wore them till they fell off their back. Probably 75 to 80 percent ended up in rags in dustbins."

Gotcha. Twenty percent of forty or fifty shirts? Eight, maybe ten, Anarchy shirts in existence. *If they were well cared for.*

Furthermore, the stenciling didn't look right to McLaren. The stitching didn't match the way the stitching was made in the '70s. The textiles weren't what McLaren and Westwood used—not the original flimsy muslin. The buttons weren't correct. Back in the day, the duo sewed on pearl buttons that were then hand-painted, dyed, and then striped with a brush. The buttons would have no holes in the front, just in the back.

Perhaps this was evidence that only a punk aficionado might know—minutiae interesting only to collectors, fashionistas. Certainly before an actual bidder went to the auction to spend x (insert hefty amount) number of dollars, that person might have checked out the photos of the clothes or known something about the detail.

However, you didn't need to know this to sense, on some level, something wasn't quite right.

Because three things stuck out: One, the preview included things in sizes that were wrong for the era. Two, the preview included items that just sounded, well, too new. Three, the preview included things McLaren was sure he'd never made.

It doesn't take a collector of clothing to say to oneself, *That's true, Sid Vicious was pretty skinny!* If you personally were in the preview, after you'd contemplated how the shirts might look on your wall or on yourself (*what, this old thing?*), the thought might have crossed your mind, *I'm the same size as Johnny Rotten?*

And remember, two or three short years. Made in the kitchen. How many items could be left? Picture with me the image of punk kids meticulously washing, drying, and storing their beloved clothes in a climate-controlled facility. Hmm.

Even if McLaren had gone blind, which he had not, there were no answers for the issues of size and the vast quantities of available punk garments in the marketplace. Practically available to any layperson on any corner.

Who among us has not tossed out some item of clothing only to say later, "Boy, I wish I still had . . ."?

The logic follows:

Very short period in time = rare access to that circle = very few artifacts left over from that time

You don't need McLaren's opinion to ascertain if items are authentic. The detail is right in front of you.

Herein lies the difference between clothing and the *Mona Lisa*. The ease of identifying real from hoax in clothing is no secret, having even been parodied in popular comedy.[12]

In the 2001 movie *Serendipity,* Kate Beckinsale's character comments on the quality of her friend's Prada fake, "Eve, that's a horrific knockoff! At least my knockoff says 'Pradi,' yours says 'Prado'!"

Clothing is different from the *Mona Lisa*: Da Vinci isn't around to point to the painting and say, "It is mine/it isn't mine," but up until April 2010, McLaren was. And Westwood still is, at the time of this writing. Though she has often stayed out of the conversation, having moved on, as it were, to other creations and efforts in her life, Westwood and McLaren were in harmony when it came to the fakes. She did not raise the giant stink he did, but she agrees to this day that vast quantities of fakes are being traded.[13]

Pat Frost, director of textiles for Christie's, rebuffed McLaren, insisting that the auction house had the real deal. "Malcolm McLaren hasn't handled the pieces. I didn't see him but evidently he came to the preview in New York and saw just three or four that we had on display. As you can appreciate, the punk era is not exactly when good records were kept, but anything we have any doubts about we pull out. That's in part why there haven't been many pieces of Westwood on auction in general."[14]

Except that Frost is wrong; there have been many auctions of Westwood/McLaren clothes. Just two months after the Resurrection auction, Christie's itself had another sale that included punk items.[15]

Resurrection's Mark Haddawy also expressed bewilderment: "I don't know that Malcolm would be the best judge of what clothes were real. He was the conceptual end of that partnership; Vivienne was the designer. There's far more interest in stories that have some kind of drama, it wouldn't make a very good story if it went 'Malcolm McLaren saw these things and thought they were great.'"[16] Except that's exactly what would make the auction noteworthy; an endorsement or in-person authentication would drive up prices.

After the sale, Young Kim, McLaren's longtime assistant and partner, wrote to me about the items in the collection.[17] She said, "Ms. Westwood was not the designer in those days. Mr. McLaren was. She executed his designs and contributed to them as a co-designer. He was the designer and visionary. When the partnership broke up, Ms. Westwood's clothing designs went in an entirely different direction—away from pop culture and music and into historical costume where she has made her mark." [18]

Kim was upset for McLaren. She had taken photos of the fakes in the presence of Pat Frost, but McLaren's reputation as a great arch twister, one who loved a good story and thought it was all part of the fun, was haunting him.[19]

It happened that this particular sale was largely clothing, but collectors of the original Westwood/McLaren clothes are often culture collectors: punk aficionados or culture hounds after a particular era in time. Sales often include posters, records, pins, and other memorabilia.

To that end, these sales further continued the legend of McLaren, as influencer, rock icon, designer, and so forth. Indicating nothing was left from the era but dust in dustbins would have been a resounding death knell to punk culture worldwide. To what end did he benefit by dismantling them?

Whether Pat Frost or Mark Haddawy actually believed that McLaren could no longer recognize clothes he had made himself, and the larger question of why McLaren would quiet his own legend weren't the key, however. The off-sizing, the newness, the wrong materials: What stood out was that this was evidence a layperson could readily see.

Pulling the thread on this auction unraveled a much bigger ball of yarn. If Christie's was authenticating fake clothes, what supposition could be made about the arts and antiquities? Would they really risk it all over some old shirts? The Christie's story was part of a much larger web that has the potential to call into question items in museums around the world.

Let's talk about how questionable items might find their way into museums: provenance.

Here is a standard path any item might follow to enter a museum:

> Owner obtains an item. → Owner seeks a letter of authentication. → Item and letter are presented to auction house. → Auction house accepts the item for sale. → Press, catalogs, and bidders set a price on the item. → Sale of the item (or its inclusion in a sale) sets an asking price (unsold items are catalogued both in printed books and online archives with an expected price range). → Item is then viewable in permanent catalog (regardless of whether sold) and can be referenced. → Provenance of item is no longer in question. → Seller cites auction on CV as proof of legitimacy to museum. → Seller is successfully added to the short list that museums list as "trusted" sources.

Pressure has been on museums worldwide to capture a piece of punk history. So much so that a few items were already housed at the Metropolitan Museum of Art in New York.

Before the auction, in July 2008, McLaren had been quoted in the *New York Daily News* column Rush and Molloy as saying that the bulk of a collection of Westwood garments—which controversial contemporary artist Damien Hirst had purchased from vintage-clothing dealer Simon Easton—were fakes. In the piece, Easton refuted the claims, saying that McLaren "rewrites history constantly."[20]

Malcolm explained: "[Sellers] try to naturally gain provenance by getting some old has-been rock star and they get them for twenty or thirty bucks to sign something saying they wore this shirt. I know members of the Sex Pistols who did this! Then you find out that Damien Hirst found out that Steve Jones, the guitarist for the Sex Pistols, simply lied! After selling to Christie's, Easton was able to sell to the Metropolitan Museum, and that's how fakes ended up in AngloMania [a 2006 Costume Institute exhibit]."[21]

The Costume Institute has in recent years taken front and center at the Metropolitan Museum. Thanks to *Vogue* and its editor, Anna Wintour, the exhibits have become a splashy, annual, red-carpeted, black-tie ball, attended by celebrities from across the world, covered by fashion magazines, general interest newspapers, and television. In fact, Wintour has been so influential in bringing attention to clothing that in May of 2014, the museum renamed the wing, the Anna Wintour Costume Center.

"I informed Andrew Bolton and the head of the dress department, I wrote in great detail and they acknowledged the letters . . . but after the exhibition," alleged McLaren with regard to the Westwood items in the AngloMania exhibit. "Easton has an eBay site called punkpistol.[22] He's even gotten Rizzoli involved to do a punk book,[23] so then he would even have a book showcasing the fakes as real! The Metropolitan is too embarrassed."

Of the articles in the Metropolitan Museum's 2006 exhibit, some are said to be without question because the museum says they are purchases it made during the 1970s directly from the Vivienne Westwood store.

I am a bit skeptical of this. Let me see if I get this right. Back in the '70s, when Johnny Rotten is yelling onstage, the museum's acquisition arm has the prescience to go out to a no-name store in West London and buy up handmade shirts made in a two-year period, having intuited that they'll be culturally significant later? Especially given that until Anna Wintour's diligent efforts, that wing of the museum was treated like the insane relative relegated to the cellar?[24]

But okay. I'll give it to them. Leaving those items aside, at least seven articles in the exhibit came from Simon Easton.

If McLaren was right: Easton bootstrapped his fakes *successfully* into New York's venerable Metropolitan Museum of Art.

Or at least Rizzoli thinks so. After hearing doubts about Easton, they quietly put the publishing of the coffee-table book on ice.

When I first connected with McLaren, he was at that moment breaking the bad news to artist Damien Hirst. Hirst had spent more than \$160,000 with Easton on the goods and subsequently written to Malcolm asking him to authenticate.[25]

In 2008 and again at the time of the writing of this book, I called on the Metropolitan Museum. In 2008, museum spokesperson Nancy Chilton told me that Andrew Bolton would write me an e-mail. Subsequently I got a call saying that the museum would decline to comment. Nothing in writing. This time around, my calls went unanswered. Many of the Westwood items remain part of museum collections.

Why wasn't the museum banging down my door to make sure I—and everyone else—knew that they wouldn't accept a fake?

Perhaps they didn't need to. Because the sale went forward and all the items sold. There was ample opportunity for the general public to have developed some doubt going into the auction, even among those who knew nothing about the punk era. In addition to customs officials across the world, McLaren had sounded the alert to rare-book dealer Glenn Horowitz and Horowitz's manager, John McWhinnie. Journalist Paul Gorman had written about it on his website then and even became involved in helping the police with identifying the fakes. *The Daily News* had reported it. I had written about it in the *Financial Times*.

Many people along the way were alerted *and* continued to turn a blind eye. Why?

Let's give the Met, Frost, Haddawy, and Easton the benefit of the doubt and say that profit was not the motive. Let's say they genuinely believed. Resurrection's Mark Haddawy had said, "I've spent twelve years searching out these pieces."

We know that as a store owner, he could certainly tell the difference between "small" and "extra large." But after over a decade of hard work searching out the collectible items, would he want to be told he'd wasted his time or, worse yet, made a bad purchase?

After Damien Hirst purchased the clothing, he didn't call on Malcolm McLaren because he was looking to establish the truth—he'd *already* bought the clothes. Rather, he was looking for evidence that he had made a good purchase.

This is a psychological phenomenon known as *confirmation bias*. Once we've made up our mind about something and made a decision, we have a deep need to be reassured that the decision we made was the right one. We have an inherent need for certainty, and that need is activated by important decisions. So instead of keeping an open mind and admitting all the evidence, we selectively seek out evidence that will confirm our original decision.

Consider this: Marketers at research firm Millward Brown cite examples of car buyers. When it comes to awareness of car advertisements, conventional wisdom would point to a heightened awareness of car ads *before* purchasing. However, studies find that consumers are most aware in the three to six months *after* the purchase of a new car. Why is this? New car owners want to be assured of having made a great purchase. Once you've spent, you're checking the messages in the marketplace. No person is so insecure as the person who wants to be told that he or she made a great choice.

If you've ever turned on *Antiques Roadshow*[26] or any other of the myriad TV shows where consumers take various possessions to antiquities experts to be evaluated for worth and authenticity, watch the faces of the owners whose items are deemed to be worth less than they'd originally thought. Their hopes have been undercut.

This hope—in its aspirational variant—is mocked in an episode of the old sitcom *Frasier*, called "A Tsar Is Born."[27] Frasier and his brother Niles are initially embarrassed by their father's desire to go on *Antiques Roadshow* with a hideous bear clock that was owned by their great-great-grandmother. But their attitude changes when it's discovered that the clock is worth $25,000 and might link them to Russian royalty. However, their social-climbing ladder is rapidly broken when it transpires that their ancestor was a maid who stole the object from the rightful owners. To add insult to injury, their father has already spent the not-yet-earned $25K on a Winnebago touring van, the absolute antithesis of any vehicle the Mercedes-Benz- and BMW-loving brothers might want to be seen in.

Spoof or not, even those who are not aspirational are vulnerable to this need for reassurance. My own mother (sorry, Mom!) is a great example of this targeted evidence-seeking. Ever since she and my father bought their home back when I was headed off for college, she has never failed to peruse the real estate pages. When signs pop up around the neighborhood for open houses, you can guarantee my mother will make a little visit. Is she looking to trade in her beloved home? Maybe, maybe not. I do know that she is evaluating the properties around the village. What are they worth? What are they going for? Are house prices going up or down relative to the worth of her home? In short, did she pay a good price? And does she still have a good deal on her hands? Mom with her anxieties is certainly not alone.

We want so badly to believe that we will play our part in the con.

And still, confirmation bias doesn't explain it all. Sometimes some of us want so badly to have been there that we will tell ourselves a little white lie—or worse, a great lie.

It follows that:

"It was a massively influential period in recent history" = with any massively important time period, people want to have been there or to say that they were.

McLaren himself understood the deep desire to believe and struggled with shattering the illusion: "This happened to me [not wanting to admit it] in the summer in the Hamptons, where these exceedingly rich collectors of first-edition William Burroughs books, etc., are obsessed with buying punk memorabilia, and it mainly consists of buying these very rare handmade T-shirts, and they're prepared to pay an awful lot of money. You feel terrible because the collectors so desperately want them to be authentic. I don't like to tell them the terrible truth, and you go along with it! People who are now middle-aged who were just a bit too young and covet it because they missed it. The kinds of people who want to purchase them [now] tend to be very large and middle-aged!"

This effect of lying to ourselves even when we know something might not be authentic isn't just true with the punk years. We like to use style to rewrite history in all aspects of retro. Our desire of late for something from the yesteryears can be seen in the recent explosion of "speakeasies," as a nightlife archetype that places a particular emphasis on a bogus authenticity.

It may seem like speakeasies have nothing to do with museum fakes, but the link is this: When we begin to lie to ourselves and we participate in the lies, however seemingly harmless, we open the door to other greater, and potentially harmful, lies.

Starting with Milk and Honey, speakeasy bars have boomed in cities such as New York and San Francisco. They all seem to follow the same model: They feature bartenders remonikered "mixologists," shaking much too vigorously, and as loud as they can, vintage (or vintage-looking) cocktail shakers, pouring out high-priced cocktails with clever names such as "Say Hello to My Little Friend" (a fresh lemonade with the Bolivian coca leaf liqueur, Agwa de Bolivia) and "Bob's Your Uncle" (Thai botanical infused gin, a lime-basil-lemongrass-agave infusion, chili pepper, fresh lemon juice, soda).

Frequently these watering holes come with a slew of rules and quirks meant to conjure up Prohibition. Either you have to make a reservation (Raines Law Room or Dear Irving, in New York) or you have to crawl through a phone booth via a hot dog stand (PDT, also in Manhattan, accessed through Crif Dogs) or you simply can't stand up (The Gibson, in Washington, DC). They almost never have signs (Slide, in San Francisco, or Death and Company, in New York).[28]

Only it isn't authentic. Did speakeasies have slides, hotdogs, or cachaca? No. Lemongrass infusions? Try bathtub gin that could clean the enamel off your teeth. We want so badly to have been there, we'll buy a piece of it. However derivative or—as the marketing says—"inspired by."

Even as we all know that these aren't the days of Al Capone—which incidentally weren't nearly as glamorous as the bars above—we allow ourselves to be drawn into the illusion. Do we genuinely believe we're in the 1920s? Of course not. But quickly do a search on some of the nightlife review sites and note how many times the word "authentic" comes up in discussions of speakeasies.[29]

No one wants to research how dangerous and miserable Prohibition actually was before going out on a Saturday night—remember Debbie Downer, the hilarious *Saturday Night Live* character who managed to ruin every joyous occasion by pointing out the downside? So we agree to tell ourselves that these speakeasies resemble how it really was.[30] The crux of this, though, is that we will end up buying a piece of it. HBO noticed and set out to sell you a part of it as well—its Emmy Award–winning show about the era, *Boardwalk Empire*.

Buying a piece of imagined nostalgia via a drink called Off to the Races (a peachy version of the classic Mint Julep) costs you just sixteen dollars and is fairly harmless, but wanting to rewrite history can come with a price. Much greater frauds are allowed—and even encouraged—in our culture.

Study after study shows that many of us are less than honest with others when it comes to another kind of idealized history: our own. And furthermore, we know it.

Consider the average resume. ResumeDoctor.com, a resume advisory service, found that nearly 43 percent of more than 1,100 resumes it checked for dates of employment, job titles, and education, contained at least one inaccuracy. Nearly 13 percent of the resumes contained two or more such "mistakes." Cofounder Brad Fredericks didn't attribute this to human error. He said that job applicants think they are giving themselves an advantage by lying. Challenger, Gray and Christmas, an outplacement company, says that job applicants commonly lie about education, including listing a degree from a school the applicant didn't even attend! Other bald-faced lies include making up job titles, inflating salaries, and telling untruths about why one left a previous job.

The Society of Human Resource Managers (SHRM) says that it's even worse than that. Their studies show that over 53 percent of us lie about our resumes![31]

Consider these data they uncovered:

Eighty percent of all resumes are misleading.
Forty percent inflated salary claims.
Thirty percent altered employment dates.
Thirty percent included inaccurate job descriptions.
Twenty-seven percent gave false references.
Twenty percent state fraudulent degrees.

We even admit we're willing to do it. When college students were asked in the same study by SHRM, over 70 percent said they would lie on their resumes to land their dream job. The con isn't being called, because too many have something at stake in it.

The difference, though, between resumes and shirts is that someone spent a great number of man-*years* to show we lie on resumes. That is, to observe what SHRM is telling you, you would have needed access to hundreds or thousands of resumes. You would need to fact-check them as Equifax or Challenger has done. You would need to do a study. Meanwhile, clothing provides this instant study every day of your life. In front of you are those hundreds and thousands of data points, aggregating in your subconscious every day.

This is also the difference between fakes in general and fakes in clothing. The Metropolitan would be far from the first art institution to have its items called on authenticity. In January 2016, the Knoedler Gallery went to its first trial of what will sure to be many. The gallery sold thirty fake paintings as pieces by Pollock, de Kooning, and other Abstract Expressionists. At the heart of the lawsuits is whether the gallery knew, or worse yet, is involved in the forgeries.[32]

Forgery is also pervasive across many kinds of gallery and museum items. When the watch company Vacheron Constantin first had a look at the Metropolitan Museum's vintage watch collection, it found fakes, many from hundreds of years ago. Yes, as long as items have been expensive, people have been knocking them off!

But the McLaren items were a bit different. Only the most trained eye might be able to see the difference between a good de Kooning and a fake, a real Vacheron and a forgery, but anyone could wonder out loud whether the Seditionaries shirts were just a bit too . . . large.

Let's take an item of clothing even closer to home. You don't have to go to the museum. Just open your closet. Have you worn jeans this week? What if I were to tell you that they might be fakes? This isn't so outrageous. A number of years ago, I broke the story on counterfeit denim.

Circa 2000, three LA-based guys, Michael Glasser, Peter Koral, and Jerome Dahan, changed the jeans industry forever. They took what had previously been a weekend staple that hadn't seen much change in approximately four decades, and invented premium denim. What was $35 was now suddenly $200. And with the price hike and crazed demand, came the fakes.

In fact, this very data point in front of my eyes was how I came to write the article. One Sunday, I was shopping in Manhattan's Union Square when I came across a street vendor selling suspiciously cheap 7s. I quickly snapped up two pairs, at forty dollars each, and ran home to find a contact at 7 for All Mankind.

"When I was growing up, there were those Rolex watches that everyone knew weren't real and of course now designer handbags, but this is the first time I've ever seen denim on a folding table on the street. Never before," Jeffrey Laytin, 7 for All Mankind's trademark attorney at Sullivan and Worcester, told me.[33]

The company was so plagued with counterfeits that it had to invent a woven code into the content label, a detail they felt would-be thieves could not reproduce.

The news article bothered people. Sure, no one likes a fake. Much less when it involves that emblem of All-American apple-pie-ism, jeans.

But a lie about denim is important not because it's a great retail story; it's because all of us own a pair of jeans. All of us do not own a real Vuitton handbag, but we all own jeans. The denim market, according to The NPD Group, is approximately 450 million pairs sold each year, which means that if the pair you currently have on are fake, you are part of a lie at this very moment, a lie so innocuous that it has made its way into your everyday.

That was why the article rattled people. There is no greater threat than the lie we live with every morning.

The observation of that clothing around you is an observation of human behavior. And the deduction of it would have led you to the same conclusion as to why people lie on resumes—and that people will have convinced themselves that some of the lies are true. However, you would not have needed to commission a $100K study. In this way, clothing offers you a front-row seat as it reveals the inner persons of others and provides the ability to act on this knowledge so that you are *ahead* of the game, not *waiting* for the big study.

Contemplate how many times today you've seen a fake handbag. When I initially wrote about the McLaren auction in the *Financial Times*, my editor remarked to me that what separated this story from all the other tales of fakes—be they the questionables on Canal Street or the quite good copies coming out of the Dubai marketplace—is that no one was putting those knockoffs in a museum. But weren't they? Wasn't that precisely what was happening?

When what we believe is more important than what is, everything changes. The 2007 Davenport Lyons report, "Counterfeiting Luxury," indicated that one in eight consumers bought fakes. No surprise there. But the report went on to separate lookalikes from fakes. Purchasers of lookalikes weren't going to trade up and become luxury consumers. But, surprise, "Fake buyers are luxury consumers; in fact, they are more likely to buy genuine product," according to the report. And only "half of all fake purchases were made in the mistaken belief that the product was genuine." Meaning that at least 50 percent of fake buyers not only knew the items were fakes but were okay with it. And they were—and are— buying the real deal as well.[34]

That is, you can stick a few fakes in the auction if everything else is real.

In 2004 and 2005, Korean scientist Hwang Woo-suk rocked the scientific world with his claims that he had succeeded in cloning human embryonic stem cells. Washington-based journal *Science* received Hwang's first paper in mid-March 2004 and rushed to publish the findings a mere two months later. Though the magazine said that the findings were put through the same process as a whopping twelve thousand other papers received that year, the paper was fast-tracked, published faster than other submissions to the journal.

In the paper, Hwang and his team claimed to have successfully created an embryonic stem cell using the somatic cell nuclear transfer method. Then in May 2005, they claimed another breakthrough—that they had created eleven human embryonic stem cells using 185 eggs—and it was published in the June 11 issue of *Science*. Unfortunately, both papers contained fabricated data, and Hwang's studies were found to be fraudulent.[35]

How did this happen? Hwang had the proverbial previous sale: He claimed to have cloned a dairy cow, as well as a BSE-resistant cow, before claiming to succeed in cloning humans. Furthermore, Hwang had the right CV. He was a professor of theriogenology and biotechnology at Seoul National University and was widely considered a pioneer in the field.[36] And *Science* was under tremendous pressure to acquire the piece; if it had not been *Science*, then *Cell* or *Nature*, the two other leading journals in the field, would certainly have been interested.

Science's executive editor, Monica M. Bradford, was quoted as saying, "We work on the assumption that the data are real."[37] The publication of the papers was a debacle for the reputable *Science*, and it came at a quantifiable cost. In May 2006, Hwang was convicted of embezzling millions of dollars.

Yet none of this has stopped him. Later that year, Hwang opened a facility, Sooam Biotech Research Foundation with private funding from fans. And despite his 2010 conviction being upheld in 2014 by the South Korean Supreme Court, approximately 50 percent of Sooam's funding now comes from government grants.

Whether Hwang is a determined scientist is not the debate. As of December 2014, he has successfully cloned hundreds of animals, dogs, pigs, coyotes, and cows. What is up for debate is whether his research can be trusted. Or more importantly, why we believed so firmly—and continue to believe—such that we cannot let a hero fall.

Confirmation bias.

These stories indicate that what people want to believe to be real versus counterfeit is all in the perception.

After Hurricane Katrina, there was an enormous boom of people going online to websites such as eBay (where fashion has no "season"), looking to reclaim their memories.[38] After people got settled in temporary places, the next thing they tried to do was reclaim pieces of their lives. One survivor rebought the dress her sister wore at her wedding reception. It was the wrong size, and she didn't even have a permanent address at which to receive it, but in her mind, it even superseded the "shelter" element of Maslow's three needs that we talked about in chapter 1.

Hurricane Katrina had another unexpected effect on the fashion industry. It wiped out whole reserves of natural skins: crocodile, alligator, and lizard farms. As a result, in the years after, fashion saw a great leap forward. Earlier, faux had looked fake and real had been, well, real. And to some extent, no one in fashion wanted that gap to be bridged. After all, why would anyone pay for luxury if the knockoff could be had for one tenth—no, forget that—one *hundredth* of the price? But Hurricane Katrina changed all that. Designers simply had to find a way to make fake snake, fake crocodile, and even fake ostrich look real. The result is that today, with the best fakes, even luxury sellers can't tell the difference. In the aftermath of Katrina, fashion was instrumental in wiping out an occurrence everyone wanted to forget.

But that anecdote is more than a retail shift. And McLaren is more than just a fascinating conspiracy. People infuse clothes with meaning. And in some instances, fakes will do. This need is so desperate that it permeates every level of our lives—from the jeans we wear every day to the clothing displayed in museums.

We can see in clothing the lies we tell ourselves. Superstitions may tell us early what large groups are thinking, but what about the frauds we perpetuate on ourselves? These are examples of us fooling ourselves and each other, but more than what's being faked, asking questions can give us a greater understanding of why we are choosing to con ourselves.

Clothing allows us the opportunity to question ourselves and to spot early on the frauds others are attempting to perpetrate on us. If we do spot these frauds early, we can save ourselves from financial ruin and other impending disaster.

Let us discuss something that we've all observed and been affected by: the whistle-blowers of high finance and the little they were heeded.

In 1999 Harry Markopoulos sent warning letters to the SEC about Bernie Madoff, whose Ponzi scheme would finally be uncovered over eight years later. New York University professor Nouriel Roubini said as far back as 2005 that home prices were on a speculative wave that would devastate our economy.[39] Ed Gramlich, who served as Federal Reserve governor from 1997 to 2005, wrote in his book *Subprime Mortgages: America's Latest Boom and Bust*, published in 2007, that he had been warning Alan Greenspan about the subprime mortgage crisis as early as 2000.[40] *Economist* and *Forbes* columnist Gary Shilling claimed he'd been warning since 2005 of the housing crash, the credit crunch, and the deep recession to follow.[41]

Certainly now everyone wants to claim they "knew," but some actually did. And they warned us. Why didn't we listen? Why were we so eager to discredit them? Whether the currency is triple-rated securities or punk-era memorabilia, the endorsement process follows a similar trajectory. One bank or agency claims that triple-rated securities are good, and they're then sold to another bank, by which time whether they were any good to begin with, is moot.

Credit-rating agencies are now under scrutiny for having given investment-grade ratings to mortgage-backed securities (MBS)[42] based on risky subprime mortgage loans. These high ratings enabled the MBS to be sold to investors, thereby financing the housing boom.

There are indications that we are currently (2017) undergoing the buildup to another bubble—and its subsequent burst. Standard & Poor's is shaky. Housing prices are at another all-time high. Russia's economy is tremulous. China has been experiencing a slowdown since 2012. First the Federal Reserve indirectly adjusted the interest rate by withholding money that banks can loan, then raised the interest rate on March 15, 2017. Encouraging people to borrow or have access to money stimulates an economy. Rate hikes do the opposite.

All the signs we experienced prior to the dot-com burst of 2001 are here as well. In 2014, venture capitalists threw $48.3 billion into American start-up companies. In 2015 that number was even higher, $58.8 billion, making it the second highest full-year total in the last twenty years.[43] In the fourth quarter alone venture capitalists put $11.3 billion into 962 deals. The fourth quarter was also the eighth consecutive quarter of more than $10 billion of venture capital invested in a single quarter, which equated to funding at levels that haven't been seen since 2000. A report called the "MoneyTree Report," from Pricewaterhouse-Coopers and the National Venture Capital Association, based on data from Thomson Reuters, and documenting these 4,356 deals has caused concern among a handful of naysayers. And it should, because although the actual number of deals were up only 4 percent as compared with 2013, forty of the investments were classified as "megadeals," those of $100 million or more. Twice as many as the previous year.

At the July 2014 Delivering Alpha investment conference, some brave venture capitalists cited tech stocks as heavily overinflated.[44] Duquesne Capital's Stanley Druckenmiller went so far as to indicate that 80 percent of companies recently pursuing an IPO have no earnings. But others silenced him.

Perhaps the most concerning sign has been the money received by Uber, the on-demand car service. In 2014 it was said to be overpriced, having raised a whopping $4.9 billion including $1.6 billion in debt financing on January 21, 2015.[45] Yet when institutional investor Peter Thiel criticized Uber as overvalued, he was immediately dismissed by many others, including Benchmark's Bill Gurley, who has invested in Uber.[46] The company's valuation has since skyrocketed to $51 billion after a total of seven rounds of funding of $7.4 billion since its launch.[47]

And yet the company's planned (at the time of this writing) IPO is eagerly anticipated. Capital markets investors are still bullish about it.[48]

At some point, someone who is brave enough to say something speaks up to voice concern or even make accusations—in the cases of art or mortgages—of fraudulence, but is silenced. And the reason no one wants to listen to that person—be it Thiel, Markopoulos, or McLaren—is that people don't want to be told their purchases are not worth what they believe—especially if they may want to sell them in the future. The situation becomes—in the true sense of the phrase—one of mass hysteria.

BANKERS' WIVES ARE LAUNDERING MONEY

YOU'RE A rich banker working at a Wall Street firm or a hedge fund manager in your high-rise office overlooking Central Park. Among your perks? When you have as much money as you do, your wife doesn't have to work. She cares for your kids, oversees your household, and manages your social life. You see very little of her because of the hours you keep, and your marriage has suffered as a result.

Your wife's credit card bills come in every month: Bergdorf Goodman in Manhattan, Harvey Nichols in London, Joyce in Hong Kong. You pay the bills for her shopping without thinking about it, in part because of the guilt over growing apart. You wonder if one day you'll come home just to be served divorce papers.

Despite your success, you long for the days when you were young and fancy-free, but now the kids are in private school and your country house always seems to need repairs. So you keep working. Bringing home the proverbial bacon. Maybe after work, you pop into a local watering hole, the kind with an oak bar and brass fixings, and you drown your sorrows in a series of increasingly expensive bottles of scotch. You wonder whether she will run off with her trainer, whether you'll become a cliché. You'd be sad for what's lost, but at least you know that with the prenup, postnup, and bank account she doesn't know about, she won't get everything.

But what if I were to tell you that your wife was laundering your money? Clothes-laundering it, so to speak. She goes to the stores, she buys clothes that you pay for, and then, without clipping off the store price tags, she cabs it up to a posh uptown boutique and drops them off, where they are promptly resold for half their original price. The consignment store writes your wife a nice little check. And she pockets the money, building up a little reserve that neither you nor your high-priced lawyers will ever be able to touch.

All this is actually happening down on Wall Street, on the Upper East Side, in Greenwich, and over in the City in London. The practice even has an icon. When Jackie Kennedy married her second high-profile husband, the Greek shipping tycoon Aristotle Onassis, she lived in fear of him taking his money and running. So she notoriously bought hundreds of thousands of dollars of clothes and promptly dropped them off, unworn, tags still on, at the Manhattan consignment store Michael's, which flipped the merch and wrote Mrs. Onassis a hefty check every month. Mr. Onassis paid the bills, the store pocketed their commission, and none was the wiser for the little laundering that led to a nice (and totally legal, I might add) nest egg for Jackie.[1]

If Jackie's story had been an isolated anecdote, it could have been argued that her habit was symptomatic of the fear experienced by just one vulnerable high-society woman of being deserted and left destitute. However, in late 2007, as the subprime-mortgage crisis started to break, the above practice started to spread. Like an unstoppable infection, consignment stores reported women arriving in droves and off-loading clothes.

When I told this story to the head of communications at Goldman Sachs, I'd never seen a man more eager to run off and tell his colleagues. And my story, when published in the *Financial Times Weekend*, lifting the veil on this escalating trend, did indeed alarm husbands all over the world, and it sent them scurrying home to examine their marriages (and closets).[2]

There's a reason that I'm telling you this story.

The story above was indicative of something much bigger: the coming of the global financial crisis.

We've talked about how people wear their thoughts, concerns, and fears. And how clothing allows us the opportunity to question ourselves and to spot early the frauds others are attempting to perpetrate on us. Now having seen *when to look out* for clothing anomalies, and *what lies to listen for*, let's talk about some of the ways that clothing is a reflection of large movements.

We'll get back to Jackie O and all those banking wives selling their clothes, but first let's break down how the soft-goods industry reflects our zeitgeist.

In the summer of 2008, cycling became a trend in the world of fashion. In New York, the designer Cynthia Rowley, who liked to cycle to work, made a decorated bicycle and sold it in her shop. She released a matching cycling-clothing collection. Menswear designer Andy Spade got involved with the Bicycle Film Festival, a yearlong celebration of the bicycle, that traveled through sixteen cities from New York to Zurich to London then on to Tokyo and Melbourne, with movies, parties, and of course, bicycles. In Paris, Karl Lagerfeld designed cycling-themed items and attended Spade's events. Former *Tatler Magazine* beauty editor Antonia Whyatt, model Kristine Petersen, and Danish designer Louise Amstrup started a cycling-clothing line. The fashion trend even made it into denim, with Rock and Republic founder Michael Ball launching Rock Racing, a race cycling team, with matching apparel.[3]

But this didn't all occur because some designers who happened to love bicycles got together over coffee and decided.

What precipitated cycling's moment was a confluence of several factors. The first factor leading up to the rise of cycling clothing was the interest in exercising outdoors. In a study of outdoor recreation, Resources for the Future researcher, Juha Siikamäki found that per-capita time spent on outdoor recreation more than doubled in the United States from 1965 to 2007.[4] The key change was not in the time that individuals spent, but rather in how many people got involved in outdoor pursuits.[5]

A second, perhaps less visible, factor for the rise in cycling was the launch of the consumer electronics gadget, Fitbit. Founded in May 2007 in San Francisco by James Park and Eric Friedman, the activity tracker immediately received the attention of technical writer Tim O'Reilly and CNET writer Rafe Needleman. There was a reason for this attention. For the first time, we were able to not only measure aspects of our own individual health but also broadcast it to others. Let's not forget that the trend for sharing personal information with others was just about to crest. Facebook and Yelp both started in 2004, self-publishing nipping at the heels of city guides that had previously only showcased experts.[6] Fitbit became a category changer that has since spawned countless knockoffs and wearables with the company receiving $66 million in funding.[7] (Take note of this, because in later chapters, we'll talk about how wearables can save lives.)

The third factor was the rise to prominence of the first "green" US vice president, Al Gore. After leaving office in 2001, Gore, who had been involved in environmental issues since his freshman congressional term in 1976, turned his attention and, more importantly, the power of his voice, full-force to environmental issues. He founded the Alliance for Climate Protection and The Climate Project in 2006, started to help organize Live Earth concerts, and even headed the venture capital firm Kleiner, Perkins, Caufield and Byers's climate change practice. But he became best known, and environmental issues received their biggest boost, when he wrote the screenplay for director David Guggenheim's movie *An Inconvenient Truth*. While the movie received some criticism for its presentation of science,[8] the film won the 2007 Academy Award for Best Documentary Feature, along with dozens of other film festival awards. It has to date garnered nearly $50 million in worldwide box office sales and become a part of teaching curricula worldwide.

Suddenly everyone was talking about the environment.

People wanted to spend more time outdoors. People became more conscious of the environment and the impact of cars. And suddenly there was a way of tracking how much time one spent doing exactly that. How fit are you? How much time are you devoting to yourself? What is your daily role in saving the planet?

Fitness as a whole had been evolving since the 1980s, a result of aerobics; the popularization of exercising, courtesy of Jane Fonda's workout tapes; and fit-tertainment movies such as *Flashdance*, *Footloose*, and *Dirty Dancing*.

But never before had fitness also carried a message of caring.

Caring about the environment.

Suddenly cycling became the answer. Here was a way to make a small impact without actually doing very much of anything.

Remember the Lance Armstrong bracelets we discussed in the last chapter? There is perhaps no greater symbol of wearing the trend than those emblematic yellow bracelets. They came into play the very summer that cycling clothes hit the runways; the 95th Tour de France, the summer of 2008.

Fitbit and the Livestrong bracelets provided thousands with a way of speaking without speaking: *I am fit. I care about my body. I care about the environment. And oh by the way, I'm charitable.*

In this way fashion measured the world around us. But what about us measuring the world using fashion?

Let's talk about trends.

A *microtrend* is something that affects only a small group of people for a short period of time, usually in just one industry. Cronuts, acid-wash jeans, teacup-sized dogs, all microtrends. A *macrotrend* is a large, sustained shift in the way consumers behave. *Macro* because it is a trend that impacts many segments of our lives—and many sectors of industry—such as politics, societal beliefs and systems, technology, and economics.

In soft goods, microtrends are more linked to style. They might be useful, for example, if you want to know if hemlines should be higher or lower next season. But macrotrends affect other elements of the economy, even in the soft-goods industry, such as wearables. A good example of this is the Apple watch. As a watch designer, the microtrend would be whether or not you want to incorporate "smart" watch features into anything you plan to offer in the next couple of years. The macro viewpoint of this would be the impact of wearables as a whole and how the Apple watch might have a ripple effect on, say, payment systems, or how we bank.

Cycling clothing led to a macrotrend. In August 2007, the mayor of London, Ken Livingstone, announced a plan to study the city of London and implement a bicycle rental program similar to the Vélib system in Paris. It was launched in July 2010 by his successor Boris Johnson and officially called the Barclays Cycle Hire, nicknamed Boris Bikes.[9] The implementation of this program has had wide-reaching effects across the city's engineering, urban planning, environmental, safety, regulatory, and tax industries. At the time of this writing, the last estimate made by TfL (Transportation for London) was that in 2015–2016, the plan would cost taxpayers £225m (approximately $285m); by the end of May 2013, more than twenty-two million fatality-free rides had been taken.[10]

It also led to the launching of NYC's Citi Bike program in 2011. In turn, the Citi Bike program has affected the rezoning of various neighborhoods across the five boroughs of New York, including closing off large traffic thoroughfares such as sections of Herald Square, Times Square, and Union Square in Manhattan. Streets have been changed for bike lanes. Bridges have been rebuilt to accommodate bike paths, and parks have been added alongside the Hudson River. Even car traffic and its regulation, such as tolls and pricing for congestion hours, have been impacted by the Citi Bike program.

In this way, the soft-goods industry reflected a number of microtrends—an interest in the outdoors, the rise of consciousness around the environment, the ability to signify caring and health on the wrist via Livestrong and Fitbit—and in turn spawned a macrotrend that rippled through urban planning and numerous other ancillary industries.

The macrotrend was made up of small elements, all of which led to an unstoppable force that not only became the United States' largest bike rental program but changed the infrastructure of cities worldwide.

Let's take another example.

Consumer recycling of plastic really began in the 1990s. While plastic became popular in the 1970s, slowly replacing glass bottles in a variety of household items, from shampoo to detergent to soda pop, it wasn't until two decades later that lawmakers passed legislation requiring the labeling of various types of plastics. Programs to offer plastics recycling were tried; some worked, some didn't, but it was during the '90s that Americans, still the biggest consumers of plastic goods, developed the recycling system that exists today. The American Chemistry Council estimates that 94 percent of us have local access to recycling plastic.

With this shift, naturally, came fashion. In the early 2000s, clothing that announced to the world that its wearer recycled, came into vogue. Much like the Fitbit announced that one exercised, and the Lance Armstrong bracelets announced social consciousness, various fashion items now allowed you to yell loudly to the world, "I recycle!"

A company in Italy interpreted the Hermès Kelly bag with tribute versions made entirely from old measuring tapes, vinyl records, sponges, old magazines, even first-grade homework assignments. Nahui Ollin, a Mexican designer, started selling clutches made from candy wrappers. The list of designers using recycled materials in their collections could go on for pages. But while there were the usual suspects such as DDCLAB, a company that had always experimented with new materials, and the recycled-material-happy company Project Alabama, the difference was that mainstream clothing companies got in the game. In Spain, Camper shoes used partially recycled tires, and in the United States Dr. Scholl's released a shoe with recycled metal. Japanese packaging company Muji offered recycled socks and clothes, and Air Force outfitter Cockpit sold a men's "Officers Blanket Coat" made from recycled WW2 military blankets at Harvey Nichols. No doubt about it: Less was not just more; it was "in."

Saying (or showing) we recycle had become so trendy that some fashion labels saw it as more important than actually recycling. French bag company Goyard offered to monogram the recycling symbol, a triangle composed of arrows, onto its large "St. Louis" shopper totes for buyers willing to spend an extra $310. While some bloggers incorrectly reported the bags as recycled material, ads that ran with the offer clearly stated the bags were 100 percent "recyclable," not recycled. In adding the recycling logo to an existing bag, what exactly would have been recycled?

Now in their defense, the Goyard tote was environment-friendly in one way; it was naturally made, without plastic or petroleum products. The tote bag offered in the advertisement was new, made of new materials, and had a price tag of $1065—yes, before adding in the recycling logo cost. There was an irony to making new bags with the "eco" iconography.

But fashion was simply reflecting people's desire to express themselves.

In a way, recycling and its accompanying symbol had become a new generation's peace sign. The peace symbol, the most recognizable ideogram of the 1960s antiwar movement, an upside-down, forked Y inside a circle, originally created in 1958 by British commercial designer Gerald Holtom, became so co-opted by fashion that for the subsequent two decades, it adorned everything from Moschino couture dresses, Coach key rings, Christian Dior tan suede purses, and LaROK and Lucky Brand sweaters.

Inder Bedi, the founder and designer of Matt and Nat, a line of nylon bags fashioned entirely from recycled plastic water bottles, told me that it was inevitable that the recycle logo would have the same appeal to fashion as the peace symbol. "Both recycling and the peace movement are positive movements and people worldwide are looking to embrace positivity."

Who could argue with that?

Certainly no one disputes the desire for peace just like now no one can say that caring for the environment isn't good, but just as it was easier to wear a symbol than take a stance on war, so it was with recycling. There was no controversy in wearing the recycling symbol (unlike with peace, back in the 1960s protest days), but makers are still researching whether all the water and oil used in recycling plastic bottles is equal to the environmental impact of making one leather bag.

Isn't there something ironic and cynical about making and buying something that says that you, er, make and buy less?

Nonetheless, the recycling trend sold in soft goods. And it sold well. In 2008, Nahui Ollin's candy wrapper items sold one hundred thousand units across eight hundred boutiques in France, Italy, and Monaco, and at Topshop, Global Luggage, and Adili in the United Kingdom.[11]

Perhaps in the ultimate twist, Anya Hindmarch, who had released a canvas tote with the printed statement "I'm Not a Plastic Bag," deliberately marketed the carryall as a limited edition. The campaign was meant to reduce consumption of plastic grocery bags. But the company created so much buzz around the product and released so little of it that consumers desperate to snatch up the bag got into long lines at grocery stores in the United States and England. The totes, with an original retail price of a mere £5, skyrocketed to £500 (approximately $635) on eBay. The result? The campaign spawned the creation of hundreds of thousands of knockoffs. That is, more goods, more consumption. Consumers all eager to prove their "greenness" with a bag that was supposed to say "I reduced my impact by consuming less" did the exact opposite.

The controversy hit at the same time that China announced it was trying desperately to curb its carbon footprint by investing $10 billion in renewable energy. How confusing it must have been to be under economic pressure to manufacture more of a product, especially for so-called green-savvy consumers in the world's other big polluter, the United States, that says, right on the bag, that the buyer consumes less product.

Myles Levin of J Shoes pointed out that the issue of announcing and using recycled luxury goods was one of, well, luxury. "Markets that are very concerned about green are ones that are economically prosperous. If there's a huge recession, how is it going to affect each consumer's choices? There is a hierarchy of needs; it's an affluent privilege to be having this conversation. Those struggling are not thinking about what happens to their trash." Indeed, these are what we would consider problems of the First World.

In other words, the recycling symbol in the twenty-first century has indeed followed the same trajectory as the peace symbol did. Has it become so co-opted that we don't even know what it means even as we love to use it more and more?

People are willing to buy something if it has the recycling symbol on it. And why not? It makes us feel good. There's a message to the outside world: *I'm recycling; I'm good.* It is the proverbial equivalent of taking a pill that appeases all the guilt we have as a society. There's a need to tell oneself, *I'm not a bad person, because I recycle.* No one wants to think of himself or herself as bad. We're melting the polar ice caps but, hey, no one wants to be the person who killed off the polar bears. Fashion then and now is reflecting our need as a developed society to appear green at any cost. Even if it's a lie. Indeed, the soft-goods world reflected the overwhelming and tsunami-esque movement of greenness.

But what about those instances when clothing can do more than tell you about large movements after the fact? What if those large movements can help you get a jump on the macrotrend?

In my day-to-day consulting work, I am often asked what I do as a futurist. Do I look into a crystal ball? In a way, I do. That crystal ball is the amalgam of all the small ticks and movements that make up a macrotrend. What I essentially do is digest elements into something larger.

In this way, sometimes fashion trends will allow even those who know nothing about finance to sense where it's all going.

Back to the bankers' wives.

Here is the psychology of what can occur in a relationship of means. When people marry, there is an implicit contract that there will be equal roles, that each will provide a support system for the other. The agreement may not be one of equality but one of parity. I bring to you. You bring to me. We each contribute.

Then real life occurs.

We've all heard that women make on average seventy-nine cents to the men's dollar.[12] But consider the following statistics:

1. The gender pay gap is worse for mothers, and it only grows with age. It takes mothers nearly six additional months (an extra 155 days) to earn what fathers earn in just one year.[13]
2. As a result of the pay gap, women experience more difficulty paying off student loan debt.[14]
3. Women face a pay gap in nearly every occupation.[15]
4. Increased levels of education don't close the gender pay gap.[16]

Let's leave gender perception and issues aside. That's a different book. We can look at these variables solely for their economic impact. These naked facts force couples to make choices. Even those who might prefer different gender roles may find themselves at odds with the existing options. Workplaces might not favor equal leave for parents, or one job simply pays more than the other. One parent might simply decide to stay home.

Over time, whether five or ten or twenty years, the relationship becomes symbiotic. One partner might earn the lion's share of the household income where the other provides the lion's share of the support system. A recent study showed that single women do on average twelve hours of household chores a week, whereas married women with no children perform an average of twenty-one hours. (Married women with children came in at twenty-eight hours.)[17] A splashy news headline might conclude that just the act of having a male spouse adds nine hours of housework to your week. But the takeaway is also that one spouse is providing the other with nine hours of labor that adds to the ecosystem of their lives. Regardless of who picks up the socks, the agreement is that both have developed and enjoy a lifestyle together. You can't do it all without the other person.

However, in a divorce, the legal breakdown is nothing like the actuality. Contributions are measured differently. Access to money to pay bills or financial resources to pay for the divorce proceedings becomes part of the negotiation of marital assets. According to Lili Vasileff, president of the Association of Divorce Financial Planners, this is when the earning spouse—gender irrelevant—sometimes decides to become discriminatory or cruel.

"I don't want to pay for you to take the kids to camp this summer"; the defending spouse is put in the position of having to tell the kids *no*. Money becomes the power and vehicle of control, a means of negative manipulation in the divorce process. The attorneys I spoke with indicated that money is used to coerce people into custodial relationships simply because the party that holds the money can do so. In essence, money becomes both the symbol and the key to a means of survival, to pay for bills, including paying for the divorce attorney to have a just process.

Vasileff had some amazing stories. She told me of a client who would go to Neiman Marcus and rack up credit card bills. "She had no cash for groceries and she had no cash for school lunch. He said she would fritter it away." Meaning, the client's husband felt that his wife was going through cash and credit too quickly and frivolously—and this was before divorce proceedings. At the time I interviewed Vasileff, she was also working with a client who would purchase gift certificates and sell them to her friends in order to pay for her legal fees because the client did not have any fiduciary accounts solely in her own name.[18]

In sum, these were not women who were spending $15,000 at Saks just for fun. In their situations an imbalance of power that was exhibited through money was suddenly exacerbated by divorce and the anxiety that surrounds the issue.

Many articles and movies have documented the insecurity that Jackie Onassis felt. In a marriage of means but inequality, she found a way to squirrel away money and create assets in her own name, which became really important. With Aristotle, as long as he was alive she would be supported, but what if something happened to him? His assets would go to his children. Or what if he woke up and changed his mind about being with her? Jackie lived in fear that she might wake up to find there was no money in the bank.[19]

"Anxiety and insecurity that you will be destitute the next day, I hear every single woman fearful she'll be a bag lady overnight. I've never heard a man say that; it's not in the genes," Vasileff said.

Now here is the connective tissue. Counsel for those in a divorce will often instruct the earning spouse to pay for credit card bills.

Think about this. If your store credit card bills are paid, but you can't afford the legal bills, what becomes your option?

In order to make the leap from clothing to the financial implications, one has to think about the way we view clothing and the soft-goods industry. Vasileff indicates that men and women are perceived differently when it comes to certain kinds of purchases. On a divorce balance sheet, women's spending is held to a different standard.

"When men spend on a designer suit or they travel or they have tea with their employer or they have subscriptions, it's rarely examined as frivolous spending. When women belong to clubs or have designer clothes, it's scrutinized as frivolous."

In a divorce, attorneys advise the partner of lesser means not to reduce spending levels, which provide the standard at which spousal support will later be based.

Therefore the earning spouse—male, in this particular scenario—will frequently cut off access to daily living expenses but still pay for frivolities. "Why do they continue to pay the store credit cards? It enhances their image—it makes them look like a good guy—in a perverse way, it makes them look like good guys when in reality they haven't given their families anything to live on."

The research I did raised many issues around income and parity. Issues around the lifespan of women, equity versus equality, the value of housework, and so forth. What constituted a fair playing ground? What made for a dignified divorce?

But the takeaway was the same.

The men did not associate soft goods with cash, but rather image.

The women, however, saw cold, hard cash.

After all, the soft-goods industry is a multibillion-dollar business.

The higher up the earning ladder, the greater the disparity between the income of the earning spouse and the lack of income of the stay-at-home spouse. Add to this the incredible cost of maintaining a Wall Street–style household.

Wednesday Martin's "memoir," *Primates of Park Avenue,* mocks the wives of Manhattan's "masters of the universe" types, with tales of their expensive wardrobes and beauty regimens, jockeying for positions for their offspring, costly holiday destinations such as Palm Beach, and the potential for receiving "wife bonuses," an "annual salary" achieved for delivering excellent households, children, and companionship.[20] While Martin was criticized for fluid timelines and whether her book met scientific research standards, her examples are very much similar to the ones I'm providing here.

There are countless economic indicators with which to gauge the health of an economy. For example, one can track the growth of nations. The World Bank shows China's GDP (gross domestic product) growth clearly year to year, from a staggering 14.2 percent in 2007 to a slow steady rate, dropping from 9.5 percent in 2011 to 7.8 percent in 2012, 7.7 percent in 2013, and 7.3 percent in 2014, and so forth. This would indicate to you a coming slowdown worldwide of demand for luxury goods. One can also keep an eye on federal interest rates. When the Fed changes the national interest rate, it has a rippling effect on our national economy. At low rates, money is cheap to borrow. If it's inexpensive to borrow, we experience periods of growth. When the Fed raises rates, it becomes costly to borrow, ergo, things slow down. And so forth. Are homes going unsold in secondary cities such as Miami or Houston? Are technology stocks overvalued? There are ample factors to watch.

However, the purpose of taking a look at the soft-goods industry is not to replace other possible types of market analysis. What it can do is provide you with thought-provoking ideas and a different way of looking at the world. In later chapters, I'll tackle the kinfolk movement and our desire to get back to the farm, as well as the high-tech world that's coming at us—driverless cars, anyone?—and how they relate to soft goods. In those chapters, you will see how you can use these points of data—clothing—to think differently about the world. For now, consider these stories as a potential marketing and psychology tool. Another arsenal in your cadre of weapons.

Now back to those wives.

In 2008, as the economy foundered, bankers—and other tycoon-types—worried. And they brought those worries home. Their wives, in turn, worried. Much like Jackie did, they wondered what would happen should the proverbial faucet simply stop running.

A little-known fact is that divorce rates spike during poor economies. This isn't too hard to understand when walked through.

Poor economies → Job insecurity or job loss
Job loss → Home stress
Home stress → Divorce

What made the selling of clothes, and the pattern I saw with the Wall Street wives, though, was more than just the above.

The stories were not isolated incidents. This was a whole industry, not isolated to one small store, but rather a business sector. And in turn, it was actually an indication of fear in the financial marketplace. Long before it was really making the news. Women were flipping clothes in an anticipation of a shift in their personal economic situations. And the widespread practice foretold elements of a wider movement, before the movement was actually happening.

The particularly anxious behavior of finance wives wasn't just being displayed by the middle class[21] or the emergent affluent: This was affecting the truly rich. Those engaged in such surreptitious rainy-day hoarding had annual disposable incomes of a quarter of a million to half a million dollars, euros, pounds, what have you; that's half a million they have liquid in the bank, to drop on anything from movies to restaurants to holidays to gifts at any given time. These people have incomes well into eight figures and households that typically don't even feel dips in the economy.[22]

To put this into context, we're talking about households where the annual bonus pool is double the combined earnings of all 895,000 full-time, minimum-wage workers in the United States.[23]

When people with that level of wealth started panicking, it was a sign the recession would last much longer than originally expected, and maybe even turn into a depression.

You had but to go to the stores to see this firsthand.

NOT SHOPPING COULD SAVE THE PLANET

"A PAIR OF never-worn Costume National shoes, a Burberry women's navy blazer, Vanessa Bruno summer-weight pale-pink cotton pants, Armani pants for both women and men, and vintage mink fur coats." These are the designer items one woman says she acquired without paying. Not a single penny.

The history unfolds as follows. On May 1, 2003, Deron Beal, a Tucson, Arizona, resident, sent out an e-mail to about thirty or forty friends and a handful of nonprofits, suggesting a network of recycling goods. The idea was simple: He would set up an online message board where people would post, item by item, things they no longer wanted, for others to take. No one would sell anything and no barter would take place, but simply by giving away something unwanted to someone who did want it, Beal and his friends would keep still-usable goods out of landfills. Beal called his website Freecycle.org—the word *recycle* blended with *free*. The website grew rapidly and now, from antique claw-foot tubs to appliances like washers and dryers to designer clothing to old PCs, through events from New York to Helsinki, everything imaginable is swapped.[1]

Today, the world is at your fingertips. The saying "There's an app for that" has never been more true. You can swipe right for a date, a restaurant, send flowers, summon a car, even book to stay in a total stranger's home on the other side of the planet.

But back in 2003, when "Freemeets" began, there were no apps. To put it into a technological timeline perspective, they started a year before Facebook was founded.[2] Remember those brick-sized cell phones Motorola put out? They had gray screens with a bunch of numbers, and texting someone involved hitting the correct number key to toggle to the selected letter. Imagine if you had to fax someone to get that freebie. Just wait with me while the dial-up sounds. It wasn't that bad, but . . . almost. I tell you this to give you some sense of how unstoppable something has to be to continue to break through communication barriers.

Which Freemeets did. It turned into a worldwide phenomenon, one that now spans a whopping 75 countries with over 5,289 local groups totaling more than 9,115,672 members worldwide.[3]

The numbers are staggering.

Of course, it would be easy to say, "Who doesn't like the idea of free stuff?"

But there's a greater reason that Freemeets got this big and a more important reason why I am telling you this story.

That free stuff could save our planet.

Let me explain. In the future, the bottled water you love so much could cost one hundred dollars for a tiny bottle. I am not trying to scare you. This is a real figure.[4] We've all heard the oldie but goodie, "Water is our most precious resource," but unfortunately this isn't some trope trotted out by hippies; we are actually running out of clean and usable water. Love Rio? Mercury lead and aluminum have washed up onto the shores of Brazil. Fancying a trip to Capri this summer? Species in the Mediterranean have been eating garbage and their own waste to avoid poisoned algae. Live in LA? In 2020, you won't have enough drinking water.[5] Craving sushi? Eating a small amount of fish from a contaminated waterway is even more dangerous than drinking water from the contaminated source for one hundred years. Bad night out at your local bar? Diarrhea kills over 2 million people every year.[6]

But what if changes in the way we think about or consume clothing could change our world—such as keeping safe drinking water available?

Regardless of where you stand on environmental issues, there's no denying that there is a dialogue taking place about carbon footprints, chemical dumping, and how we can save access to water. In 2015, the United Nations Climate Change Conference, COP 21, was held in Paris in an attempt by nations to limit the degradation, deforestation, land use, and runoffs affecting our planet, including the polluting of seas in the Philippines.[7] This is an area of particular concern because UNESCO feels that our food begins with the plankton, coral, and fish that grow in those seas. It was not the first conference of its kind by world leaders; the Kyoto Protocol in 1992 was an earlier attempt by nations to manage global warming.

The clothing industry is the largest polluter of fresh water, after agriculture. The World Bank thinks that 20 percent of the world's industrial pollution comes from textile-dyeing and runoff from the process.[8] There's also a much-cited statistic in the fashion industry that it takes 1,800 gallons of water to grow enough cotton to make one pair of jeans.[9] Some even think that number could be as high as 2,800 gallons.[10] The reason this statistic is often quoted is that if you go by the belief that you should drink eight eight-ounce glasses of water a day to stay hydrated, those jeans are the equivalent of one day's drinking water for approximately 5,600 people.[11]

Playing an enormous part in the discussion is not just the making of clothing—though fast or "disposable" fashion speeds up the cycle of pollution[12]—but also the upkeep of clothes we already own. Part of the pollution is also in the care of your clothes postpurchase and how long an item's life cycle is.

The average Californian uses 181 gallons of water on average in just one day, a significant portion of which is on laundry.[13] According to an American Water Works Association Research Foundation study, 21.7 percent of indoor water usage in homes comes from washing machines;[14] in other words, maintenance. Water may play a large part in the creation of our clothing, but also a large part afterward, in the usage of it.

The reason I seize upon California is not just its consumption levels. California is also the state with the most severe drought in the United States, with 2015 being the fourth year of extreme drought conditions. The state's third driest in 119 years of records was 2014, according to a US Geological Survey.[15] That condition led to Governor Brown's executive order of a statewide 25 percent reduction in water utilization, with hefty fines for those who exceeded their daily quota of water.

What was the immediate impact?

"I launder in bio friendly soap; do laundry as little as possible by wearing clothing 2-3 times. I use gizmos in the dryer to shorten the cycle." (Anne-Marie Boyce, San Francisco).

"Let my sheets go for 2 weeks; I wear scrubs at work so can really cut back on laundry" (Margaret Mann, San Francisco).

"I worry about the water consumed by washing clothes in my 25-year-old washing machine that uses a lot of water, so I'm very careful about adjusting the water level for each load" (Renée Flower, Santa Cruz).[16]

These quotes from a *New York Times* article were part of a discussion on how California residents have adjusted to water restrictions in the state. In addition to making adjustments to their bathing and cooking regimens, they changed their approach to clothing.

In other words, access to water changes how people handle clothes they already own. The behavior wasn't driven by brands, nor did it necessarily come from an ecoconscious consumer. It came down to a fear of being fined. Households afraid of being levied washing fines also ran out to the laundromat. Ironically, the laundromat industry has seen a rise in business ever since the record-making drought began.[17] Beverly Blank, president of the Southern California Coin Laundry Association, reported that instead of washing at home, consumers would run out to pay-laundry facilities in an end-run around potential fines.[18]

Fine-dodging aside, this is clear: The drought of the last five years in California shows an inextricable link between clothing and water. If we lose access to water, we care for our clothes differently. Any shift in our clothing consumption patterns, therefore, has the potential to impact how we use water.

So could we look at it the other way around? How can clothing be used to change our future? What impact would we have on our environment if suddenly we didn't rely on water the way we did? What could a future look like where inventions in fashion could, in fact, save the planet?

This is not hyperbole. Runoffs from washing our clothes pollute the ocean. In Indonesia, the Citarum River is considered one of the most polluted rivers globally. This is largely due to the textile factories on its shoreline, which have dumped mercury, arsenic, lead, and other toxic waste into the river. Greenpeace tested the water and found high levels of lye-based drain cleaner, capable of burning skin. But more importantly, the water tests positive for nonylphenol, deadly to ocean life and a disruptor to the human endocrine system. Here's the kicker: Clothing produced with nonylphenol remains in garments, coming out only after a number of washes. Therefore, nonylphenol ethoxylates are effectively coming out when we wash our clothing. While banned in imports and manufacturing in the European Union, nonylphenol has not been banned in the United States.[19]

It is hard to understate the environmental impact of runoffs into our oceans. In 2015, I wrote a piece about the pearl-farming industry in the Philippines. The reason those seas matter so much is that many ecologists believe they are ground zero for our delicate food system. Slash-and-burn cropping (where land is burnt and then crops are grown in a fashion that destroys the land) has been used to provide rice for the country. In the rainy season, the runoff destroys coral. The destruction of coral, which controls carbon dioxide levels in the ocean, has led to rising sea levels.

While this runoff is not from soft-goods-related chemicals, it has very much the same effect.

In addition, cyanide fishing has also decimated the area. Fishermen use cyanide to put fish to temporary "sleep" by anesthetizing the nervous system, allowing the capture and transport of a still-living fish. However one teaspoon of cyanide kills one kilometer of coral. And cyanide is one of the chemical runoffs from the soft-goods industry.

So in order to save water, do we just stop washing our clothes? Do we dry-clean instead? Machine-washing uses fewer chemicals but consumes fuel and a staggering amount of water. And there are the runoffs. Dry-cleaning, on the other hand, pollutes in an entirely different way, since an overwhelming majority of dry cleaners use petrochemicals—to such an extent that the chemicals cause cancer and kill off entire ecosystems, yet saves on H_2O.

"And then there is the chemical used by the vast majority of cleaners . . . about 85% of dry cleaners now use perc," went a 2005 article in the *Guardian*.[20] "Americans spent more than $7 billion on dry cleaning last year, but . . . long-term exposure to very low levels of the chemical [perc] will cause cancer," stated a 2007 piece by CBS.[21]

Consumers are becoming well educated about the potential risks of petroleum-based solvents used by dry cleaners, namely tetrachloroethylene or perchloroethylene, commonly called "perc," as shown above. A solvent that had been widely adopted by cleaners to replace CFC 113 (a chlorofluorocarbon banned for its effect on the ozone layer), the Environmental Protection Agency had issued warnings against acute and chronic issues resulting from exposure to perc. Issues such as liver and kidney problems, and cancer.

But what if there were an alternative altogether?

In 2009 I wrote an article about this. The backlash against chemicals had driven consumers away from dry cleaners. Designers were looking for solutions. How could they make clothes that would bypass the pesky after-care problem of dry-cleaning? What if we could invent machine-washable black tie?

Designer Tadashi Shoji was using memory taffeta for formal dresses, which allowed for machine-washing of ball gowns. Ermenegildo Zegna was investigating how to make a machine-washable men's suit. Cashmere company Loro Piana was looking into fiber treated with nitrogen. The total solution wasn't quite there yet. In theory, soon you may be able to throw a ball gown or a suit into a washing machine and have it come out structurally intact, via a system that will neither pollute nor consume excess water, but in practice, the issue remained: removing perc didn't solve the water problem.

There are a number of possible (and potentially competing) futures presented to us by clothing and in the next chapters we'll talk about agribusiness, novel fabrics, and new inventions, but for now, continue to follow me on this journey of the impact of Freemeets. How could we solve the problem of water? What if there is a third way altogether?

One possible future is reflected in our growing interest in just consuming less.

You see, free was not the only reason Freemeets grew and has now grown so large. If "free" alone was the impetus, then the clothing donation bins that now sit unguarded in supermarket parking lots would have been looted long ago. Rather, the site was in the vanguard of changing the way people consume and the way they communicate their consumption to each other. People wanted to find a solution. They wanted to communicate their interest not just in fashion but their desire to reuse, to each other. Those who were exchanging through meeting on Freemeets were part of a shift that was just beginning.

When I first wrote about the company, the idea of swapping or selling or thrifting (thrift store aficionados have indeed turned it into a pastime and a verb), was still on the periphery of consumer attention. The sort of thing that would be mocked in an episode of *Portlandia*, the scripted television show making fun of hipsters. But put aside any notions you may have that this was something taking hold on the fringes or that it was desperately crunchy.

But the Freemeeters were onto something that might help save the environment, whether they meant to or not.

Because within a handful of years, Freemeet started to go corporate. Read: luxury.

In the summer of 2008, credit-card clearinghouse giant Visa got into the game. Visa rented a temporary space—in retail lingo, a "pop-up store"—in London's Knightsbridge neighborhood, down the block from Harrods and Harvey Nichols and a slew of other top-end, high-priced retailers, and set up a little swap of their own.

And they weren't offering up pee-stained items you might find at the Goodwill. We're talking Chanel and Prada, all on hand for people to take for . . . no monies exchanged. The involvement of actress Lindsay Lohan, who at the time was still riding high from her box office hit *Mean Girls*, was a coup for Visa. She brought in items from British designer-favorite Giles Deacon and Miu Miu and even lent her face to promotion of the event.

If the idea of Lohan or any A-list Hollywood actress rummaging through bins at your local 99-cent store is unimaginable, that gives you some sense of how far swapping had come in just five short years. Costly castoffs from Lindsay for free, just down the road from stores carrying those very same brands where one could pay for a four-thousand-dollar skirt with a Visa card? Yes, there was something distinctly ironic about the whole affair.

The event was so popular—they literally ran out of items in the first day of the four-day event (and had to rustle up some donations lickety-split)—that the following year the company took out an even larger space in Covent Garden. Simon Kleine, the head of corporate communications for Visa Europe at the time, told me that it was simply about engaging consumers who enjoyed fashion. Perhaps he thought a little empty space in the closet might be filled with a new purchase or two.

However, swapping had become more than just an opportunity for Visa to get in the faces of the style-conscious. In the research for the article, I found numerous sites dedicated to swapping: SwapStyle, Swap-o-Rama-Rama, Clothingswap. That was just the beginning.

Freemeets was a harbinger of things to come, much in the way that eBay was.

Think about how eBay was perceived when it began. Do you remember it as a place for oddballs seeking vintage clothes? Today, however, eBay functions much the way a big retail corporation might. This is due to the sheer numbers that eBay draws and the volume of transactions it processes. Brands that initially underestimated eBay's retail impact eventually had to take a second look at the Internet giant.[22] Labels such as BCBG and others ultimately shifted to an "if you can't beat them, join them" mentality toward the selling channel, and they now partner with the site. It is so established that you can even buy a new Mercedes on eBay.

The persistence of eBay as a round-the-clock shopping option has revolutionized the seasonality of clothing—you can buy a winter coat from five years ago if you like! In recent years, fashion designers have abandoned the notion of runway shows previewing collections that won't be available for months in favor of immediate ordering. eBay has a large part in this; why wait six months when you can find something online at any time, middle of the night or otherwise? eBay has even changed how people make payments with its payment arm, PayPal.

In essence, something that appears to be niche can have tremendous impact if it grows large enough. Similar to eBay's eventuality, the size of Freemeets started to lead to changes in the way people sought out goods and, as you're about to see, changed both the way people continue to seek out goods and the goods that are available to them.

The retail world was taking notice of what had heretofore been a rogue movement, a living room trend, but Visa and celebrity involvement also heralded something larger: a focus on how fashion should be consumed. Women (and men) might still want to refresh their closets, but how we are doing it had already started to change. The notion of not buying new, or even . . . not buying at all (gasp!) had started to take hold.

I am sure this led to panicked boardroom meetings at big clothing companies. For years, we've been pummeled with the idea of constant refreshing and constant shopping. "New for Spring!" "Summer Swim!" "Back to School!" "Holiday Party Dresses!" Consumers had been complaining that what was once twice-a-year shopping had turned into four times a year had turned into eighteen new collection announcements.

The fast-fashion retailer Boohoo.com recently told me that they receive new goods sometimes as often as weekly. That's fifty-two times a year you should be shopping!

But when we start down the path of asking what we buy, we inevitably are led to the question of what we create.

Let us consider the size of the soft-goods industry.

The US apparel market is the largest in the world. It is about 28 percent of the global total with a market size of approximately $331 billion.

Clothing store sales in the United States total $250.7 billion.[23]

Apparel and accessories in e-commerce retail total a revenue of $60 billion.[24]

Any slowdown in consumption, if it took hold en masse, would eventually eat away at some—if not a significant—portion of this.

Households were already changing the way they shop. Consider the stores one frequented in the 1980s and 1990s. It might surprise you to learn that Target Corporation was in fact founded in 1902 by George Dayton in Minneapolis. Today, its collaborations with fashion designers feature celebrities and the occasional sellout stampede, but this was not the case in the last century. Teen shoppers would have been horrified to be dragged there for school clothes. It wasn't until 2003, when the company struck a partnership with Isaac Mizrahi, that the high-style/low-cost concept was born. In the early years, though, items from the collaboration were plagued with customer complaints around quality, and pieces could be found on the sale racks.

But by 2006, when Target launched with British bag designer Luella Bartley, it was ready to dig in for the long run. In 2009, the company scooped up Rodarte and Alexander McQueen, two design teams one would have never pictured having anything to do with supermarket fashion.[25] And the collections started to rocket out the door. Target offered early shopping via in-person pop-up stores, to invitation-only crowds, and the stock would inevitably sell out.

What changed in those ten years that allowed for the canny collaborations? Patterns of shopping changed. Today stores that would have once been viewed as embarrassing places to shop are no longer viewed as such. It is considered astute to pay less. Not just to buy less, but both pay less and buy less.

At the same time that Freemeets and the notion of swapping was starting to catch on, overseas stores such as Primark in the United

Kingdom were making inroads into households. Similar to Target, Primark had been around since 1969, but public perception around the clothing retailer was that it was cheap—not inexpensive, but cheap—and a last resort. In the mid-2000s, that started to shift. As consumers sought out ways to spend less and consume less, magazines started to feature the British "high street," or places to "get the look for less." Supermarkets such as Aldi and Lidl, which had been sneered at by consumption snobs at their launches, started to be viewed as smart choices. Grocery giant Asda got into the fashion game with the launch of a clothing collection called George and quickly cornered the school-uniform shopping market. Where previously families spent a fortune to purchase private school uniforms, the supermarket began to deliver inexpensive options, now termed "cheap and cheerful" collections.

Buying less suddenly became a mark of smarts.

By 2009, a slide show from management consultants McKinsey & Company showed that consumers perceived the price of goods at hypermarkets (supermarkets that might also sell home goods, apparel, and furniture, and contain pharmacies or banks) to even be higher than that of traditional retail discounters.[26] That is, consumers believed that there had been an improvement in the quality of nonfood items available alongside their groceries.[27]

It certainly didn't hurt that Target dressed celebrities in their collaboration collections and pushed the images out into the celebrity weekly magazines and established fashion endorsers such as *Vogue*. Even actress Diane Kruger is wearing Peter Pilotto for Target? It must be okay!

The pattern of how consumers shopped started to shift. Going to a store like Target became the first stop. Higher-end boutiques became the occasional splurge or top-off, perhaps once or twice a year. Another analysis from McKinsey's retail division shows that where consumers once considered shopping a hobby and bought lots of things, some of which were unnecessary, these days the new consumer focuses expressly on purchases of items they really want, even on basic goods or private labeled items.[28]

The clever consumer rummaged like Lohan or, better yet, found a way to get it, if not free, then for less.

Coupon sites such as RetailMeNot, exploded into the consumer consciousness, and couponing came out from behind the shadows. Saving pennies became hip as even glamorous labels such as Victoria's Secret sent out mailers for free panties promoted by scantily clad supermodels clutching balloons or frolicking on St. Barts.

In recent years, a slew of recycling resale sites have popped up, including Vaunte, Tradesy, TheRealReal, Threadflip, ReFashioner, Poshmark. The industry has grown so quickly that Tradesy has even acquired one of the smaller companies, ShopHers, an Ashton Kutcher–endorsed, venture-capital-funded entity. A number of the sites have partnered with splashy fashion bloggers, whose bouncy curls and perfect makeup draw in tens of thousands of chic eyeballs to the sites. A New York city subway ad promotes Rebagg as a way of refreshing one's Gucci purse collection.

More and more of those sites have begun functioning as apps. In 2014, I was even asked to spearhead the launch and marketing for one such app, which I described as the child of Tinder and eBay. Today, commercials for letgo and Close5 pepper ABC's Thursday night television shows. Articles are written about which apps get you the best money for selling your unwanted goods, such as Shpock, SellSimple, Boxes, or Carousell. Underlying this trend, though, is an idea that did not exist fifteen years ago: an endless lifetime of use for an item. When you're done with something, it should no longer go into a landfill; rather, the idea that "one person's trash is another's treasure" means no waste.

You can even sell your worn Target collaborations on eBay, sometimes for more than you paid for them!

Making gold from others' discards existed in other industries before fashion, of course. A colleague of mine has been so successful at his scrap metal business that he has to ferry himself and his family in armored cars with protection and has invested in a luxury watch company for fun. And in some industries, one literally makes gold from gold, as in cash for gold and the melting down of old, unworn jewelry into new, usable precious metal that can be recast. Gold recycling has increased an average of 6 percent over twenty-five years. Scrap gold climbed from 12 percent of the total gold market in 1990 to 27 percent in 2015.[29] In fact, 90 percent of all secondary supply of recycled gold comes from high-value materials; in other words, from jewelry.

What we resell or give away, though, has also changed. In 2009, I wrote about the glamorization of the old cash-for-gold businesses, with the launch of Circa, a jewelry consignment business that only dealt in pieces typically valued at six or seven figures. Once upon a time, those who sold off their gold were doing so at pawn shops either strictly because they were desperate for cash or because—to be blunt—the goods were stolen. This is no longer true. While actress Ellen Barkin famously sold her jewelry gifts from Ron Perelman in a very public "F---you" Christie's sale, Chris del Gatto, the founder of Circa, indicated that lots of other expensive pieces were being sold off to him. Gone are the days when old or used items—at all ends of the price spectrum—are undesirable.

These notions have so taken hold that actual clothing makers have started to embrace the shift. In 2011, Patagonia was one of the first. The company placed an ad in the *New York Times* that carried the headline "Don't buy this jacket" and read, "The R2 Jacket shown, one of our best sellers. To make it required 135 liters of water, enough to meet the daily needs (three glasses a day) of 45 people. Its journey from its origin as 60 percent recycled polyester to our Reno warehouse generated nearly 20 pounds of carbon dioxide, 24 times the weight of the finished product. This jacket left behind, on its way to Reno, two-thirds its weight in waste. And this is a 60 percent recycled polyester jacket, knit and sewn to a high standard; it is exceptionally durable, so you won't have to replace it as often. And when it comes to the end of its useful life we'll take it back to recycle into a product of equal value. But, as is true of all the things we can make and you can buy, this jacket comes with an environmental cost higher than its price."[30]

Suggesting consumers not buy their goods?

Wow. Self-sabotaging? Or smart?

Or simply tuned in to the movement? Other brands have also started to respond to this sense of buying less. In 2015 TJ Maxx, HomeGoods, and Marshall's, all owned by TJX, decided not to promote Black Friday, the big day-after-Thanksgiving retailer push for the holiday season. The company ran a television ad suggesting that viewers focus on relaxing and "only wrestling for pumpkin pie" instead of wrangling goods.[31] Similarly outdoor store REI closed all of its shops with a social media campaign hashtagged #optoutside, encouraging people to spend the day outdoors instead of hitting up stores.[32] Patagonia CEO Rose Marcario even followed up the previous campaign by publishing an article in the online magazine *Quartz*, suggesting that the most ecofriendly items are the ones already in your closet.[33]

In other words, maybe the answer to the water problem is just to not shop. Fewer things equal fewer problems. Consider the popularity of Marie Kondo, a Japanese closet organizer who has spawned a near cult-movement of cleaning out one's closet.[34]

So what happens when the consumption cycle changes so dramatically? What happens if we stop buying new things? Buying less, using longer, spending less money, all of it has an impact. It has the bigger potential to bleed into other economic areas and other industries. It also has a worldwide effect.

There is a term that has been floated heavily among consultants since about 2007: the circular economy. It is basically the notion of recycling. Taking as much from the making process and putting it back into the system of reuse, such that waste by-product is reduced or even completely eliminated. Some proposals suggest that adopting these kinds of principles have not just an environmental and social impact but could also turn out an economic benefit, such as an extra €1.8 trillion for Europe by 2030.[35]

Recycling has been discussed since the 1970s;[36] however, the notion of removing the "take-make-dispose" system and entirely replacing it with a total-capture system could in theory have huge effects on food, housing, and employment. In 2012, the average European used sixteen metric tons of materials. Sixty percent of discarded items ended up tossed in landfills or incinerated. The average European car is in use only 8 percent of the time, 31 percent of food is thrown out, manufactured assets last only nine years, and offices are in use just 35 to 50 percent of the time, including during working hours.[37]

At this point, however, recycling systems are fairly imperfect. Materials recycling and waste-based energy recovery achieves only 5 percent of the original raw-material value. Even successful recycling areas such as polyethylene terephthalate (PET, which we will discuss in the next chapter), steel, and paper lose 30 to 75 percent of material value in the first-use cycle.

So what about the notion of "just less"?

Consider how that might affect the world if this idea starts to catch on in the world's largest economy, China. It is expected that China will continue to expand over the next five years by $2.3 trillion. That is larger than the entire real GDP of Germany or Great Britain.

However, in early 2015 I wrote an article about the slowdown of the luxury watch market in China. What surprised me while writing it wasn't the slowdown itself. I'd known it was coming for a number of years, in significant part because of the stories above. What surprised me was how many people did not know. But if you read the first chapters of this book, you would have known as well.

China's boom economy was at an all-time high; its annual growth according to the World Bank reached a staggering 14.2 percent in 2007. It was, by all accounts, not going to last. There has been no economy that has held that level of growth for a sustained period of time in the history of the world. The following year the figure dropped below 10 percent; by 2012 it was 7.8, and it has continued to drop ever since. The current estimates for the upcoming years are in the sixes. Still, a growing economy. By comparison, the United States hovers in the twos: 2.3 percent in 2012, 2.2 in 2013, 2.4 in 2014. The United Kingdom is similar at 2.2 in 2013 and 2.9 in 2014.[38]

Now, the timeline of China is an anomaly. To understand why this is so, it is important to separate out two issues. One is that while the rest of the world had started to slow down, everyone who described China compared the economy to that of the United States during the Industrial Revolution. One great leap, so to speak.

Chinese consumption decreased from around 51 percent of gross domestic product in 1985 to 43 percent in 1995, down to 38 percent in 2005, and to 34 percent in 2013. Consultants argue that this is not a problem because household income will continue to rise, as will discretionary spending, that is, non-necessity items such as movie tickets.

The second issue involves distinguishing between manufacturing and services. In spring of 2016, Apple announced that its growth in China was slowing. This is due to a maturing market of consumption. Goods then convert to services. I have my phone, now let me buy texting. Optimists and consumer product companies are counting on the middle class growing, and it doesn't hurt that consumption is strong among millennials, rising at 14 percent every year, whereas the older generations continue to show restraint. But without government stimulus boosting the economy, experts believe that if, say, 30 percent of capacity is cut across China's overbloated industries, an approximate three million workers might lose their jobs.[39]

Companies that ramped up for China's growth will need to ramp down.

All economies go through a similar evolution:

Industrial revolution → Nouveau riche boom → Established money, quieter wealth → Conscious shopping

Essentially a leap-growth economy will never last. As economies mature, bursts of wealth stabilize. For example, first-time homeowners have now bought; they no longer need homes. Therefore, construction companies experience a slowdown in the housing market, because fewer new buyers are entering the marketplace. First-time watch buyers or cell phone owners or car consumers are a much larger group than the number of folks who want a second car or to become watch collectors. The economy slows down.

Further, when we first come into wealth, we want to flash our new toys. We want everyone to know that we can afford new toys, and we want those new toys to be as flashy as possible in order to communicate our fabulous new wealth. As we get used to being able to buy things, we feel less urgency about broadcasting our arrival. Shopping becomes something more private, more for ourselves. Eventually, having the luxury of choice on our hands, we reflect inward. What are we buying? Should we be buying it?

Consumption in China has been managed not just by culture and income level, but also partly by deliberate policies by the government. An artificially low currency makes imports more expensive, and the absence of consumer credit (bank loans, credit cards) until recently made managing consumption by the government essential.

The twelfth and thirteenth Five-Year Plans made clear an intent to pivot toward consumption by increasing the minimum wage, putting consumer protections in place, and so forth. Government officials have openly spoken of a consumption economy and encouraged spending and lending.

But this is likely to be a short-term effect. Environmental consciousness has already started to come to China. Consumers have started to notice carbon footprints, supply-chain issues, and waste.

On June 30, 2016, China pledged to reduce carbon emissions relative to the size of its economy by 60 to 65 percent by 2030, increasing the commitment of cut levels. In 2009, the country had set a goal of reducing emissions per GDP by 40 to 45 percent from 2005 levels by 2029. At the date of the new commitment, levels are down nearly 34 percent, which reflects a move toward a service over a manufacturing economy.[40]

While consumption might continue to grow, due chiefly to higher household incomes and a shift to services, consumers and the government are already thinking about the impact. It's clear that the next step will be buying less, washing less, and reusing more.

In other words, even as the consumer class in China continues to grow by the hundreds of millions due to income and to urbanization, this may drive services, but eventually we will get to some kind of peak material demand (e.g., steel consumption has already peaked).

I attribute Greece's dilemma to the fact that its exports comprise less than 10 percent of its GDP (as opposed to the rest of Europe, where the average is approximately 25 percent). And when we look at China, its growth can in part be attributed to how much it has exported over the last ten years (say, from around 2006 on). Current reforecasting of its growth has to do with a slowing growth rate—and consumption—and this in turn affects the world economy.

As the country starts making less, this will have a large worldwide impact. What will happen when Freemeets of China begin?

Where this fundamental shift starts inside the individual household—*What am I, the individual, doing?*—if a lot of individuals are suddenly making the same choices, the effect becomes something that is not only felt locally but starts to ripple out into other aspects globally.

Any movement with significant numbers can lead to significant impact.

Every day the challenges of clean, available water become greater.

Of the 71 percent of the Earth's surface that is water-covered, the oceans, that is, salt water, makes up 96.5 percent. Only 3.5 percent is fresh water in lakes and locked up in glaciers and the polar ice caps. Of that fresh water, 69 percent is ice.[41]

According to the Department of Environmental Protection at nyc.gov, every eight seconds a child dies from water contamination.

Ten thousand people die every day from water- and sanitation-related diseases, for example, from the 1.5 million people who get hepatitis A annually.

Approximately 1.3 billion people have no access to clean water, and 2.4 billion people have no access to sanitation services.

One third of the world's people do not have access to waste disposal.

Twenty-two percent of the world lives in China, and 80 percent of its waterways are too polluted for consumption.

Seventeen of the world's fastest-growing cities with populations over 10 million are in developing nations.

Sixty percent of disease is caused by deficient water supply.[42]

Consider the potential impact now of one less pair of jeans. Remember, that's drinking water for one day for 5,600 people. That's the population of Powell, Ohio, or Avon, Colorado.

Now take the 9,115,672 members of Freemeets and multiply that by one pair of jeans. That's 51,047,763,200 people who have drinking water for one more day. Or the whole world will have drinking water for fifty more days. Therefore, what impact on water could we have if we all just stopped buying things? Consuming less may just save our planet.

IS YOUR COTTON SHIRT CAUSING STARVATION?

NOMA, A restaurant in Denmark, gets one hundred thousand reservation requests each month.[1] It was 2016's coolest place to dine on the planet. At least according to *Vogue*,[2] the *Guardian*,[3] the *Boston Globe*,[4] the *Telegraph*,[5] *Food and Wine*,[6] and of course *The Michelin Guide*, which has chimed in and given it two stars. Helmed by chef René Redzepi, the spot that the Copenhagen's government publicizes with paroxysms of delight[7] made waves with something called "foraging" cuisine.

In blunt terms, it's the gathering part of "hunting and gathering" that we so colloquially think our cave-dwelling ancestors might have done. Go out into the forest, see what you can garner from the land, and eat only that. Reconnect with the earth by subsisting only on what it provides.

For this, you pay the whopping sum of $300 per person for the tasting menu. Wine not included.

Even if you don't mind the price, there's just one problem: Foraged foods are not all that great. For one thing, it's really complicated to find safe, edible foods. The most famous case of foraging gone wrong is perhaps that of Chris McCandless,[8] the wanderer who was so attracted to the concept of living off the land and walking wherever the wind blew that he ended his journey in 1992, dying alone in an abandoned school bus in Fairbanks, Alaska, after having eaten—you guessed it—the wrong item found outdoors.

He became immortalized in John Krakauer's book *Into the Wild*,[9] and the subsequent movie, but more importantly as an infamous cautionary tale. Alaskans, including the Tourism Board, shudder when his name is brought up.[10]

You may be wondering what foraging has to do with clothing. It is easy to think that what's on our table or that trends we experience in other aspects of our everyday life have nothing to do with soft goods. But just as I showed in the last chapters, that clothing can reflect our fears and that we can learn to read the concerns of large groups of people using soft goods, here I'll take you through how global decisions about soft goods are intricately woven with what ends up on your table. I'll show how what you are eating, and the soft-goods choices you make, reflect and have an impact on enormous global concerns, including whether or not we can adequately feed our population and sustain our world.

For the moment, let's get back to food.

Allow me to give you a sense of just how tough foraging can be. And, as you're absorbing these facts, consider how badly we want to feel connected to the earth in order to take these risks.

The Audubon Society's *Field Guide to North American Mushrooms*, a photo book for identifying the fleshy bodies of fungi showcases over seven hundred varieties.[11] Ones that are deadly can look alarmingly similar to ones that are served on the everyday dinner table. The world's deadliest mushroom, the death cap, can kill in just a few bites. In the buttons stage, it looks like mushrooms you find in the supermarket, otherwise known as *agaricus campestris*. At full size, it is similar in appearance to edible straw mushrooms, the *volvariella volvacea*.

When you eat the death cap, 60 percent of the toxins start to work on destroying your liver, and the other 40 percent go to your kidneys, with the whole business heading toward total organ failure followed by coma and death. Currently six thousand cases of mushroom toxicity occur in the United States. The vast majority of them are mild; there are a greater number of fatal cases in Europe, fifty to one hundred deaths a year.[12] In fact, it is believed that worldwide there are twenty thousand mushroom species identified but up to one million unnamed, potential species. But the chance of you courting death when you eat an unknown mushroom is increasing, as death cap mushrooms are spreading.[13] In 1938 it was discovered that the mushroom had crossed from one continent to another, and in recent years it has learned to jump hosts, from the European oak to the California live oak. Essentially it wasn't always a United States native, but it is now.

Even if death were not a risk of eating food from an inexperienced forager, at a minimum, foraging can also expose you to eating chemical and animal waste, environmental hazards such as pollution or gasoline, and potential pesticides sprayed on plants never intended for consumption.

Does this sound like a good idea?

Well, it turned into an international trend.

In the last five or so years, Noma spawned a whole foraging movement. In 2013, Judith A. Stock at *Full-Service Restaurant* magazine wrote an article about the fad, highlighting restaurants in Culver City, California, and Austin, Texas.[14] In 2014 Megan Pacella wrote in *USA Today* about five foraging restaurants, from The Willows Inn in Washington to the bluntly named Forage in Salt Lake City. And those are just a handful of the spots that got on the Noma bandwagon. In fact, *USA Today* has gone whole hog, I mean, whole mushroom, for foraging, with articles such as "Food foragers find fun and cash amid the wild fungi," on January 11, 2011; "10 great places to forage for food," on September 19, 2012; "Chefs unearth the practice of foraging," on January 27, 2014; "Foraging: Picking from nature's all-you-can-eat buffet," July 3, 2014; and "Wild, pungent spring ramps sprouting into big business," April 21, 2016. Sierra Tishgart for *New York Magazine* titled her article "Into the Wild: 8 New York Restaurants Where You Can Find Truly Foraged Foods."[15]

I wonder if she knows the McCandless cautionary tale.

So why has this craze—essentially gathering bits never intended for the dinner table—and selling them at such an exorbitant cost turned into such a phenomenon? Wouldn't you like a nice filet mignon for one tenth the price? I have no doubt some will cite the influence of Michelin; Noma was awarded its first star in 2005. But this attribution is unlikely because, in the United States alone, there are at least 1,681 Michelin starred restaurants.[16] In Europe, there are a staggering 16,319. Imagine what one restaurant might need to do to stand out, with that much competition.

In fact, the phenomenon stems from a larger desire to return to the land. We should be thinking twice about foraging. But we have reached such an intense demand for a "return to nature" that people are literally putting their lives on the line. Foraging is a reaction, part of a larger social movement rejecting corporate food and big business. After the advent of packed foods in the 1950s, canned goods and microwave ovens made their way into every American home. Today you can purchase a microwave for a mere thirty dollars. Quick, fast, and easy packaged foods replaced the slow days of savoring. But within a few decades, consumers started to wonder; *What is hiding behind all that packaging?*

This started the farm-to-table movement, a term that restaurants refer to as serving food where personal relationships and personal knowledge of ingredient sources allow the establishment to help diners trace the origins of what is on their plates. It has been widely attributed to Alice Waters of Chez Panisse, who liked to cook with seasonal ingredients from local farms.[17] The concept caught on as people sought to swap out modified or overprocessed foods for natural and unaltered nutrition. Wouldn't the freshest ingredients be those that had to travel the least? And there was something pure and folksy about knowing the farmer who produced the milk you were drinking or the name of the chicken that bore your eggs. Doesn't it sound and feel good?

Our desires to return to the land and its connection with food, as well as growing questions around crops, inevitably led to people calling themselves *locavores*. The term refers to a person who is interested in eating food locally grown or produced, not brought in from long distances. Long distances being approximately one hundred miles. Credit is given to Jessica Prentice, who at the time was Director of Education at the Ferry Plaza Farmers Market in San Francisco, when she was asked in April 2005 to come up with a word for an article about local eaters for the *San Francisco Chronicle*.[18] "Locavore" was the Word of the Year for 2007 for the *Oxford American Dictionary*. Prentice says she put together "loc" and "vore" from the Latin words *locus* (local) and *vorare* ("to eat," or "to devour").[19]

It doesn't seem so wrong. Wanting to eat locally might raise some day-to-day economic questions: How does this affect grocery store prices? How does this affect real estate? What if you own property or were thinking about buying summer property to rent? Is it going to be on farmland? How far away can you be from a grocery store? Can you actually get enough produce from a local community-supported agriculture group (CSA)?[20]

But the desire for local tomatoes has much larger implications, even larger than your own personal plot of land. This low-tech movement is connected to other aspects of global business.

Until as recently as 2000, farming was the world's largest industry. Many of us who live in cities aren't aware of this, of course, but an enormous part of the world remains an agrarian society.

Farms produce both our food and our clothing.

More than 1 billion people are employed in agriculture, representing one in three of all workers, with over 60 percent of sub-Saharan Africa's workforce in agriculture. Those who are poor are more likely to be in farming, and 60 percent of all child laborers are in agriculture, which means that any changes in the industry disproportionately affect welfare worldwide.[21]

Around the time Noma opened, the public was just becoming aware of concerns around crops, in particular cotton crops. When you think of natural fabrics, is your first thought *cotton*? If so, you're not alone. Such is the awesome marketing success of Cotton Inc. In 2016 alone, Cotton Inc., the consumer- and trade-focused division of the Cotton Board, an oversight and administrative arm of the Cotton Research and Promotion Program, representing US upland cotton, recommended spending around $76 million to convince you to choose cotton.[22] Over the years many of those advertising dollars have gone to the "natural" message.

Part of that is necessary, because in the early 2000s, the cotton industry was experiencing a crisis. Cotton farmers, as it turns out, have the highest incidence of cancers of any industry in the world. Study after study was coming out from the National Institutes of Health linking cotton farming to lung, breast, and other cancers.[23] Apparently, cotton is one of the least natural fabrics you can purchase and uses the most water of any mass textile currently available. As a crop, it is challenging to grow, aggravates the land, and is plagued with pests. It uses 16 percent of the world's pesticides, more than any other crop.[24] Five of the top nine pesticides used on cotton in the United States, cyanide, dicofol, naled, propargite, and trifluralin, are carcinogenic. However, demand for cotton is staggering. For 2016, worldwide cotton constitutes thirty million hectares of land.[25] One hectare is about 2.47 acres or roughly the size of an international rugby field. So that's thirty million rugby fields of cotton.

That, by the way, is the size of Italy or Poland.

Here is the glue between textiles and food.

Labor and land that go to cotton do not go to food crops that might feed local populations. While cotton has been a high-value crop, African nations are harmed by US and EU subsidies to their own producers. While cotton crops might produce income, which can then buy food, local growers earn a fraction of the profit. Unsurprisingly this demand for cotton crops is therefore controversial when factored into the future of the African continent.

Further, chemical pesticides change soil fertility, meaning that farmland used one way cannot easily, if ever, be shifted to other crops. The health of the farmers and their future generations is obviously also heavily compromised. In recent years, nations such as Burkina Faso and South Africa and the regions of West and Central Africa have heatedly debated Monsanto's genetically modified, pest-resistant crops.[26] Gains by the Missouri-based, publicly traded, multinational agrochemical and agricultural biotechnology corporation provide a distinct advantage to the United States.

Enter bamboo. In 2007, I wrote a story about the rise of bamboo as an alternative to cotton in clothing. Bamboo, a woody grass, has long been historically used in structural materials and for food, particularly in Asia.[27] With a tensile strength equal to steel and a higher compressive strength than brick, concrete, or wood,[28] bamboo has been used in scaffolding and other applications in the building industry since the third century BC.[29] Bamboo texts were used as far back as 200 BC; examples are the Yúnmèng Qin bamboo texts, which consisted of laws and public records during the Qin Dynasty.[30] By the Ming Dynasty, 1368–1644, bamboo was already in use as clothing and, in its harder forms, as hats, shoes, and boning.[31]

It was in the late 1800s that modern uses of bamboo in clothing first began, but mostly the bamboo was mixed with wool to provide an alternative fabric. Toward the end of the last century we started to produce rayon (also known as viscose) through processed cellulose made from plant fibers and wood pulp.[32] The creation of rayon as a textile was revolutionary for clothing makers. It felt like silk, yet was much cheaper to produce and did not insulate heat, which made the fabric perfect for hot climates.

In the 1990s, manufacturers realized that bamboo could substitute for wood pulp. There was an enormous advantage to it. The largest of the grass family, bamboo is the world's fastest growing plant, growing as rapidly as three feet in a twenty-four-hour period.[33] Much like lawn grass, bamboo regenerates after being cut, which eliminates the need for replanting.

On a planet where 7.4 billion people[34] are competing for land, food, and water, bamboo grows densely, yielding sixty tonnes per hectare. Cotton by comparison yields two tonnes per hectare. Bamboo is also vital in our battling of greenhouse gases. One hectare of bamboo mitigates the effects of sixty-two tonnes of carbon dioxide per year. Comparatively speaking, one hectare of forest only mitigates fifteen tonnes of carbon dioxide per year.[35]

Sixty-two tonnes is about the annual CO emission of fourteen cars per year.[36]

In addition to growing a few feet a day, fabric from bamboo was marketed as hypoallergenic, resistant to bacteria, and softer and suppler than cotton. Oh, and it requires no pesticides. There is also the subtle, yet very salient idea that you can eat it. If it's edible, surely it can't be toxic. A dream fabric?

As concerns around cotton farming grew, it stood to reason that both farmers and manufacturers would look for alternative fabrics. Bamboo sounded great. Could a shift worldwide to this textile both free up land in Africa for food crops as well as reduce the cancers plaguing and destroying the future of farmers and their families?

Not so fast. By 2009, it was such a fad that the Federal Trade Commission sued four companies for selling rayon as bamboo.[37]

The pressure to come up with an alternative to cotton was all too much. The FTC took action against the companies for deceptively labeling and promoting clothing items made from rayon as made from bamboo. The complaints stated that environmental claims of items being produced in green processes and being biodegradable and antimicrobial were false.[38]

Some charged that the simple process of turning bamboo into usable fabric required so much chemical processing that it could not be considered bamboo in its original state. In order to process the bamboo into rayon, the process used sodium hydroxide and carbon disulfide, chemicals linked to headache, nerve damage, and neural disorders in workers at manufacturers. Even worse, some retailers were simply selling synthetic-origin fabrics as bamboo.

"With the tremendous expansion of green claims in today's marketplace, it is particularly important for the FTC to address deceptive environmental claims, so that consumers can trust that the products they buy have the environmentally friendly attributes they want," said David Vladeck, director of the FTC's Bureau of Consumer Protection. "When companies sell products woven from man-made fibers, such as rayon, it is important that they accurately label and advertise those products—both with respect to the fibers they use and to the qualities those fibers possess."[39]

Remember that people were starting to ask questions about the world around them and about their consumed goods. Where does my clothing come from? What is high-fructose corn syrup? Who is Monsanto? What exactly are blood diamonds, and what is happening in Africa? The greenification of our consumer culture was leading us to seek out better labels and question the path of what ended up in our closets or on our tables. But were we able to ask enough questions?

In the end, numerous retailers, including Nordstrom; Bed, Bath & Beyond; and JC Penney had to pay out hundreds of thousands of dollars in fines.[40]

It wasn't just the FTC that threw down a major stumbling block for bamboo.

Those who support the use of bamboo as a textile often cite the fact that the crop requires no irrigation, making it a great alternative to cotton. But the process of making bamboo into fabric wasn't only heavily chemically driven; it also uses a lot of water (our most endangered resource, as we saw in the last chapter).

Manufacturers have not stopped looking for eco-friendly processing alternatives such as that with lyocell, which is used in the manufacturing of Tencel.[41] Greenyarn, a Boston-based company, is just one of many experimenting with alternative processing to make bamboo fiber.[42]

It is conceivable that we could find a better process and solve the problem of converting a dream crop into a dream fabric. But right now, it's just a dream crop. Fifty years ago, we could not have imagined today's current demand for cotton. If we do not solve the processing problem, and bamboo continues to be a chemical process that consumes water, what happens then if ultimately demand for bamboo outstrips that of cotton? Have we simply replaced one problem with another one?

We are desperate for options. People do truly want alternative fabrics and solutions that allow us to get back to the earth we knew. Today's world is in such a state of technological evolution and fast-paced change that, frankly, some people are just sick of it. There's now a National Unplugging Day and an unplugging movement, where you simply reject your technology.[43] Faisal Hoque has a three-minute read on Fast Company that encourages you to unplug at least once a day.[44] Or if you can handle longer, the website also has an article about how Baratunde Thurston quit the web for a whole twenty-five days,[45] and a step-by-step guide to totally unplugging.[46] Yes, it lives on the Internet site of a magazine about technology. Ironically.

But sometimes, as we saw in previous chapters, we are so desperate for those solutions that we are willing to fool ourselves. We will go to any length to believe that our actions are contributing to our goals. Do we want so badly to be green that we will simply buy rayon and call it bamboo? Do we want so badly to feel connected to our land that we will eat a mushroom that might kill us?

We know from the story about the Anya Hindmarch bag that I told you in chapter 3 that buying more does not mean saving more. Buying is buying. In essence, we know that it is not simply about some amorphous big corporation lying to you about rayon; the change we need to make is greater, and there is no shortcut.

The problem with the choices we are making between crops and textiles is that we are not necessarily thinking them through.

Working through the bamboo issue, if demand rises, water becomes scarcer and the price goes up, so we can also ask ourselves what the water or other environmental implications would be if this next-gen crop causes geopolitical battles in China the way cotton has caused struggles between nations in Africa. We already saw in chapter 4 that worldwide we are dealing with Sisyphean issues around water and water usage.

The last ten years have been consumed with concerns about the planet, and they, at the same time, are at war with our growing demands and needs as the world population expands. According to the Pew Research Center, a think tank, the global population is expected to increase to 9.6 billion in 2050. That's a 38 percent increase from 6.9 billion in 2010.[47]

Bamboo was, of course, not the only proposed alternative fabric by clothing makers. As people considered going natural and foraging, along with the ramifications of pesticides in everything from clothing to food, *organic* cotton became popular.

By the time of the fourth annual Organic Exchange Farm and Fiber Report in 2009, organic cotton production was growing at a staggering pace. That year it jumped 20 percent over 2007–2008 to 802,599 bales grown on 253,000 hectares. Today organic cotton is a $15.7 billion market, up from $3.2 billion market in 2008. In 2009 alone, that market increased 35 percent to $4.3 billion.[48]

But in the early aughts, those seeking a solution had limited options; some had something of a similar reaction to today's locavores and wannabe farmers.[49]

Let's look at one particular man's journey. In February 2005, Danish designer Peter Ingwersen decided he couldn't trust the organic claims of the fabrics he was sourcing, so he and his company, Noir, traveled to the sub-Saharan countries of Africa looking to grow their own.[50] They reached out to Benin, Tanzania, Kenya, Ethiopia, and Uganda through their Scandinavian-based ambassadors. Uganda was the only one to reply. Ingwersen flew to Kampala to meet with the Cotton Development Organisation. From March to September of 2005, he ran a pilot program of farmers to produce organic cotton just for Noir.

This was less easy than it sounds. In recent decades, Uganda, though not as poor as neighbor Malawi, has been contending with all the challenges facing developing nations in Africa, from electricity shortages to a military accused of abuses. Hundreds have been killed since 1998 when President Yoweri Museveni, and the government's Uganda People's Defence Force (UPDF) clashed with rebel groups, including the Lord's Resistance Army (LRA).[51] While the country also faces what most African nations are struggling with, a huge AIDS problem combined with insufficient medicine and care, Uganda in particular has an uphill battle as it has faced controversies with The Global Fund to Fight AIDS. At one point tuberculosis and malaria grants to the country were suspended over mismanagement of the monies, a huge problem since a whopping 2.8 million (65 percent) of new AIDS infections occurred in Africa, home to an estimated 24.7 million HIV-infected people. The Ugandan Cabinet is under pressure to recover billions in cash lost in the scam.[52] As if all that weren't bad enough, at the time Ingwersen decided to go grow his own cotton, President Museveni, accused in the past of high-level corruption, had just been yanked back into the spotlight over money transfers to Kampala businessman Hassan Basajjabalaba through the Bank of Uganda. This was the land into which Noir wandered with the hopes of developing and creating a luxury company. In other words, the only country responsive to Ingwersen's innovative attempts, was one already fraught with challenges.

Is this the length one needs to go to in order to get organic cotton?

More importantly though, Noir is not just a story about one company or one person or even one nation. The challenges faced by Ingwersen shine a spotlight on the enormous geopolitical and financial issues faced by anyone who may choose to follow the complex supply chain of our soft-goods crops all the way to their source—and then try to change their origins. But Ingwersen did not care. He simply believed there was no other way to truly find organic cotton. At least not at the level he personally could trust.

Now Noir's clothes are great. But they are also, really, really expensive for most people.

Organic cotton sounds great. It also costs 30 percent more than regular cotton. The reason is there's just that pesky problem: the very reason cotton wasn't organic to begin with. To get a ton of cotton requires all that water and all those pesticides. So say you get those organic cotton jeans, how sustainable is that? How much organic cotton can we really make? For a planet of 7 billion people, of which cotton represents a whopping 50 percent of our textile needs? If we try, how much land would that take? Land that could be used for food. Some of the things we think sound great when it comes to saving the planet, might not be that great. Today organic cotton is just .76 percent of cotton.[53]

In a way, Ingwersen was just like the foragers. He so felt the need to have the right solution, that the only way was to go to the source. Effectively he was one of the first in soft goods to do his own "farm-to-table" movement.

Asking questions about clothing crops and asking questions about food crops have eerily mirrored each other. Around the late '90s, the time we started asking questions about fabrics, people had started hearing about genetically modified crops. News around golden rice engineered to mitigate vitamin A deficiency hit the news in 2000. Brief history of GMO crops here: In 1935 Russian scientist Andrei Nikolaevitch Belozersky isolates pure DNA. Fast forward to 1973, University of California–San Francisco, Assistant Professor of Biochemistry Herbert Boyer develops genetic engineering or recombinant DNA, in essence man-made DNA, or rDNA. In 1980, the US Supreme Court allows the patenting of genetically engineered organisms. In 1992, Flavr Savr tomatoes, the first GE food crop, is approved by the US Department of Agriculture. In 1995, the US Environmental Protection Agency approves the first insecticide-producing crop, and the following year, herbicide-resistant crops are introduced.[54]

Google "GMO" and you will get hundreds of websites dedicated to promoting or stopping genetically modified foods. The debate is passionate and fierce. Environmentalists call out big agriculture companies as profit-mongers, theologians argue against messing with nature, scientists argue that humans have been altering genetics for tens of thousands of years. My favorite line is the one in a Harvard study about beagles that glow in the dark. Never mind the fact that neither GMO wheat nor oats are yet available on store shelves, that yellow rice is still being tested, and white strawberries are white because of radiation, consumers became and continue to be afraid they aren't being told the truth about what they're buying.[55]

Alice Waters and numerous other chefs, such as Thomas Keller, Edna Lewis, and Dan Barber had been farm-to-table cooks for a couple of decades, but suddenly everyone wants to eat at a farm-to-table restaurant.[56] And it isn't that different from Ingwersen's instinctive reaction.

At this point, you might also be wondering if a few tomatoes can really have a worldwide effect. Consider the following.

From 2007 to 2012, speculators driving up the price of corn as a feedstock for biofuels such as ethanol caused a food crisis in developing countries.[57] There is perhaps no better example in recent years of us choosing between crops, and the result of that choice, than this ripple effect. In December of 2007, the United Nations Food and Agriculture Organization (FAO) announced that food prices had risen 40 percent that year as a result. Jacques Diouf, FAO chief, was quoted as saying it was a serious risk that could impact people's access to food, aggravate food insecurity, and lead to a "food crunch" that would disproportionately affect developing countries and poorer populations. By July 2008, the World Bank was indicating that biofuels had forced food prices up by 75 percent.[58]

Things continued to get worse. Two continued spikes led to riots in 2008 in Haiti, North Africa, and the Middle East.[59] *Forbes* energy reporter William Pentland even blamed biofuels for worsening uprisings in Arab countries.[60]

It is undeniable that famine, malnutrition, and food insecurity exist worldwide. Even small changes in pricing for those who are at risk mean life or death. Some 795 million people in the world do not have enough food. That's one out of every nine. Two thirds of Asia is going hungry. Sub-Saharan Africa is the region with the highest prevalence (meaning a percentage of population is hungry and one in every four there is undernourished).[61] Malnutrition is the cause of 45 percent of deaths in children under five: 3.1 million children each year.

Now consider whether you want to use that land to grow corn or cotton. And you can see the implications. Say I am a local cotton farmer, do I try to convert my lands to organic cotton? Is this even doable? Can I compete against large subsidies or big corporations making pest-resistant cotton? Do I decide to stop growing cotton and start growing wheat or corn? Is it even possible to convert cotton farms into growing crops?

Further, a shift to one fabric and choosing it or not choosing it could shift the future of whole continents. When fashion wants to shift from one crop to another or starts making clothes out of bamboo or alternative fabrics, this means real shifts in agriculture with real implications on a global level.

Remember that clothing in the United States alone is a $331 billion economy. And that worldwide it is about $1.182 trillion. This means that any portion of this economy shifting from one textile to another can have far-reaching implications. Every day we must choose. Do we grow textiles or food? What if we can't grow enough textiles for alternative fabrics, as the bamboo/rayon fiasco proves? We can see what could take place at a larger world level, potentially changing the future of African economies, and our whole agrarian—and nonagrarian—society.

If the topic of ethanol and famine feels like a much larger or esoteric problem, consider the following microaction and its impact.

After the popularity of avocado toast on Instagram—and this falls under "Can't Make This Up"—led to a surge of an additional ninety-six thousand households buying avocados, there arose a crime wave of more than forty large-scale avocado thefts in New Zealand.[62] The demand led to a deforestation of pine trees in Mexico in the mountains of Michoacan, where locals are thinning out forests in order to meet America's love for the green fruit. According to the Associated Press, this potentially compromises not only the forests but the monarch butterfly and the amounts of natural resources involved in shipping avocados.

In July 2016, police in Morelia, Mexico, detained and seized materials being used to turn a deforested area into an avocado plot.[63] In an article entitled "The Violent Gang Wars Behind Your Super Bowl Guacamole" in the *Wall Street Journal*, José de Córdoba even equates the fruit to conflict diamonds.[64] It might shock Americans to learn that the 1,137,749,941 pounds of avocado they consume every year helps to fund the Knights Templar drug cartel.[65] But it shouldn't. The connection between our limited land resources and what we grow is deeply intertwined. With only so much acreage on planet earth, we will simply have to make choices in our crops. Biofuels are supposedly greener, but how green is it when we are decimating the Amazon rainforest?

We made choices to grow cotton, and now we have to decide if we want to grow bamboo. Do we want avocados or do we want pine trees?

There are some policy analysts who believe that we have just consumed about all we can from mother earth. In *Harvesting the Biosphere*, Vaclav Smil does intense math about how much of the planet we have consumed and how we are creating a situation for ourselves that might soon be unsustainable. For example, he says that in 2000, the dry mass of humans was 125 million metric tons. We also have about 300 million tons in domesticated animals so us plus our pets total 425 million tons. Hugely overshadowing the rest of the planet of just 10 million tons for all wild vertebrates. In essence, we had better make our choices carefully. If we do not make the right crop choices, we will not be around for too much longer.[66]

There is a problem, however, in our choices. We have knee-jerk reactions, whether in picking bamboo or foraging or going for guacamole. We often go for what sounds good. A somewhat hilarious article by Corby Kummer in *Vanity Fair* entitled "Is It Time to Table Farm-to-Table?" points out that we are now subject to "farmwashing," the idea that claiming anything came from a farm makes it wholesome and local, ergo, good, citing a series of ads called "It Begins with a Farmer," created by—who else?—Monsanto.[67]

Mark Lynas, author of *The God Species*, recently wrote an interesting blog post challenging the benefits of organic food.[68] In it he cites a study put out by the United Kingdom's Food Standard Agency indicating that—oh my—there is no nutritional benefits to eating organic over conventionally produced food.[69] He even mentions the downside, where organic bean sprouts caused some deaths in Germany. It turns out that not using chemical fertilizers puts crops at greater risk of contamination from bacteria in manure.

In 2014, the magazine *Modern Farmer* put out an article titled "Foraging Isn't All That Cool" that pointed out that the plants and mushrooms you want to eat aren't just growing right next to the walkpath. This means that even if you don't die from picking the wrong mushroom, you can disturb wildlife and damage vegetation that is crucial to our ecosystem, such as irreplaceable groundcover for birds or breeding spots for insects.[70]

We need to ask deep-enough questions. We also need to start seeing the connections of our microactions to the larger world. Just as clothing can tell you how large groups of people are feeling, individual choices can ripple out to large global effects. We need to start to see the interconnections between areas that may seem unrelated. Such as food and clothing. Or oil and cotton.

Companies such as Patagonia have been making fleeces from recycled plastic bottles since 1993.[71] In August 2015, Polartec sent out a press release that it had recycled its billionth bottle into textiles utilized by companies such as Patagonia, L.L. Bean, The North Face, Arc'teryx, Eastern Mountain Sports, Carhartt, and Eddie Bauer.[72]

PET (recycled polyethylene terephthalate) fleeces are nothing new; however, designers have not figured out how to do much more with plastic bottles than make fleece. Further, they are still working on ways we can dye this and other synthetics without water. If clothing manufacturers could turn plastic bottles into other fabrics, consider the potential impact. Plastics are made using raw material ("feedstock") from a combination of natural gas and crude oil, with natural gas supplying most of it.[73]

Natural gas that occurs under the earth is mostly methane and is used as a fuel to make materials and chemicals.[74] In recent years, we have used a controversial method called fracking to obtain more natural gas. Fracking, otherwise known as *hydraulic fracturing*, is the process of drilling into the earth and then forcing a high-pressure water mixture into shale rock to release the gas and oil contained within. The reason this is controversial is that opponents indicate the process uses tremendous amounts of water, could potentially trigger earthquakes, and may contaminate groundwater.[75] Regardless of one's opinion on fracking—and there are plenty of studies on both sides—the takeaway is that we need more natural gas and oil.[76]

We use a lot of oil. In 2015, the United States consumed a total of 7.08 billion barrels of petroleum products, specifically, crude oil that has been refined into gasoline, diesel fuel, heating oil, and jet fuel, an average of about 19.4 million barrels per day.[77] This should come as no surprise to anyone reading the news and/or watching the prices on their gas tanks. While natural gas is the primary feedstock for plastics, crude oil also plays a significant part.

According to McKinsey, plastics are an enormous consumer of petroleum, up to 32 percent of total oil demand. While that figure includes cement, steel, and some other things, it does mean that if all the plastics in clothes shifted to recycled sourcing, it could move the needle on both world oil demand and water availability (since fracking consumes and pollutes water). In 2000, fracking was responsible for only 2 percent of US oil, produced with 23,000 fracking wells delivering 102,000 barrels of oil per day. By 2014, this shifted, with the addition of fracking pumping out total production at 8.5 million barrels.[78] In fact, as of 2016, fracking produces nearly half of US oil, 4.3 million barrels per day.[79]

Ergo, shifting all fleece to recycled plastics means making fewer new plastics. Fewer new plastics means less natural gas and crude oil consumption. Which could reduce fracking. There is also the potential financial and economic impact globally. Even a couple percentage points would be huge. Fracking only increased world oil by 4 percent, and look at the impact that's had on global oil prices. We haven't shifted to total PET clothing because fleece can't totally replace cotton, but also because it just doesn't dye that well.

In the fall of 2009, I tracked the nascent emergence of a no-water dye technology called AirDye as it started to gain appeal within the fashion community.[80] One of the benefits of the technology, in addition to reducing water consumption in fashion, is that it can only be used on polyesters and synthetics made from recycled plastic bottles.

That is, if we ever figure out how to make more textiles with PET, it would effectively wipe out the need for cotton.

One designer even said to me, "This is good, because we need those fields for food."

CAN CLOTHING SAVE
THE LIVES OF MILLIONS?

MORE THAN a decade ago, in January 2005, I wrote about the watch company Swatch making wristwatches that could store ski passes.[1] Skiers could tap their watches onto a terminal and be validated to access chair lifts and slopes. If you've ever been skiing, you know that it is a pain to take off gloves and reach into a pocket. With the watches offering a form of two-way communication, it got me thinking.

What if there was a hands-free way for professional skiers to communicate with their coaches while the skiers were on the slopes? Without having to take out a device or use a walkie-talkie? Coaches could, in theory, notify skiers of changing conditions on a run or update them on timing issues.

Skiers often face dangerous conditions, such as avalanches. As recently as April 2016, Free Ride World Tour Champion Estelle Balet died in La Portale, Switzerland, after being buried in an avalanche.[2] Balet was only twenty-one and, as it happened, she was a member of the Swatch Professional Team. Matilda Rapaport, the Swedish big-mountain skier, died in July 2016 after being caught in an avalanche in Chile.[3] Avalanche deaths are not unusual; for example, the 2014–2015 snow season saw 137 deaths worldwide.[4]

Changing weather conditions matter a tremendous amount when it comes to avalanches. Warm temperatures or high winds can cause buried surface hoar, a type of frost that forms on snow, which creates weak layers that lead to avalanches. In other words, the ability to communicate changing weather conditions might make an enormous difference to the path a skier chooses to take.

The watches made by Swatch used wearable RFID (radio frequency identification) chips to store and communicate the passes. RFID is short-wave communication between two devices. Think of communication like this: There are many channels. Wireless is one form of technology that sends packets of data back and forth. Bluetooth is another. RFID is another. The differences between them are coverage range (meaning how far devices can be from each other but still be able to communicate), the frequency in which the communication operates (in what gigaherz or megaherz), whether a two-way device is used or not, the data rate (how fast the communication can be), and the applications (how given technologies can be used).

RFID technology is a communication system using electromagnetic waves. A device contacts the terminal and sends information; the terminal then receives and responds. If you've paid or ever seen a car pay a highway toll using E-ZPass or one of the other devices you put on a dashboard, you have seen RFID in action. I mention RFID in particular because, unlike other forms of communication, it does not require the users to activate the communication. For example, if you want to use the Bluetooth in your device, you first have to pair it to another device, and if you've used Wi-Fi, you know you have to scan to find a network and make an active connection to the network's terminal.

RFID is also important because it can be embedded in other wearables beyond watches and bracelets, such as soft clothing, much more easily than other means of communication; we'll talk more about how this is done in a minute.

Now, when someone is caught in an avalanche, survival is near to impossible; after forty-five minutes buried, the survival rate dwindles to 20 to 30 percent. After more than three hours, the chances drop to a fraction of 1 percent.[5] Prepared skiers bring transmitters that broadcast their location but their devices are single-direction only. What if we were able to avoid that chances-of-survival scenario altogether by communicating the conditions to the skier?

As I was working on an article about just that, at the end of 2004, something else happened.

In December of that year, Northern Sumatra experienced a massive earthquake that measured 9.1 in magnitude on the Richter scale. Three months later, the area was hit again with another one, this time a magnitude of 8.6. Respectively they were the third- and ninth-largest earthquakes in modern history. (Indonesia also unluckily has the record for the eleventh- and eighteenth-largest.)[6] The ensuing tsunami with its one-hundred-foot waves caused a particularly high death toll of 230,000 people in fourteen countries.[7]

But the death toll from many other earthquakes is due almost entirely to burial.

The 2008 Sichuan 7.9-magnitude earthquake killed 70,000 and to this day has 18,500 missing.[8] According to the Haitian government, the 2010 earthquake took 316,000 lives.[9]

So I started to wonder, what might be the outcome for an earthquake if people's clothing came embedded with RFID chips that would allow not only for rapid location but potentially hands-free communication between the rescuer and the device-wearer? In a quake, rescue workers are on a race against time to find survivors in rubble. Would the rescues have been easier and the survival rate higher in Sichuan and Haiti if RFID technology had been in place? How many more buried people might we have found and rescued or, as to the missing, simply found?

The opposite of a lo-fi world where we give up on making clothes and end up foraging for our food is one of utterly high-tech. Connected everything.

There are of course movies forecasting the perils of technology such as *Minority Report*, which fictionalizes a world where you are arrested for your thoughts, or *The Terminator*, where the machines take over for us, or *Enemy of the State*, in which a National Security official played by Jon Voight uses computer programs to frame the hapless Will Smith. And sure, we now know that Facebook and Google hold the information of millions of people. They know what you buy, what you use, where you go, who you like, what you eat, and much more.

But information technology presents another opportunity: one that assumes that since we are making and wearing clothes anyway, why not use them to their potential maximum effect? Instead of making fewer clothes, let's instead turn our garments into keys, payment systems, or even items that can save our lives.

Instead of thinking just about how clothing can tell us what is coming, let us use it actively toward improving our future. There are the messages we send just by choosing certain clothing items, and then there are clothing items that can actually send messages.

The predecessor to today's RFID was invented in 1945 by a man called Léon Theremin. He made a gadget hilariously called "The Thing," which was a listening device that for seven years hung in plain view in the US ambassador's Moscow office and, less hilariously, let Soviet agents eavesdrop on the ambassador's conversations. The Thing is considered to be the origin of current RFID chips because it sat passively until radio waves from an outside source hit it; then it was activated.[10]

The unit's descendants, today's radio frequency chips, have an incredible variety of applications. They can be used to track, manage, or communicate with everything from people to assets to animals. They can be used on books, telephones, cars, and yes, even living things. The key advantage is they can be read when a tag is inside a container such as a box or a carton. And unlike a bar code, which must be scanned individually, RFID tags can be read hundreds at a time.

In 2009 Bristol University researchers even glued RFID transponders to ants in order to study their behavior.[11] Hitachi currently makes the smallest RFID at .05 mm by .05 mm.[12] That is about the size of a speck of dust. Hitachi calls it RFID powder. Of course, the powder can't hold that much data or do much, but even a tiny tag can transmit a range of a few millimeters. This is important because the smaller the size, the easier the portability.

Now RFID tags have been around awhile. But around the early aughts, prices started to come down as use went up. Governments began to use them in passports. Malaysia was the first, in 1998,[13] followed by Norway in 2005, and the European Union and Japan in 2006. The United States started using them in 2007.[14] After mad cow disease, commercial farmers also drove up sales and drove down prices of chips as tracking livestock became a huge use for RFID on large ranches.[15] In 2004, the US Food and Drug Administration approved use for implantable RFID chips in humans, but we're getting ahead of ourselves.[16]

In essence, in the last ten to twenty years, RFID has become both much smaller and much more affordable. Tags range from about fifty cents for a ten-centimeter range, 13.56 MHz band, low-data speed card to twenty-five dollars for an active tag that can transmit as far as one or two meters at 2,450 to 5,800 MHz (or microwave levels). Simple RFID tags can sell for as low as nine cents.[17]

Uses of RFID have created convenience in other aspects outside of clothing for some time now. Launched in 1997 in Hong Kong, Octopus was perhaps the first widely used contactless payment card.[18] The city was already using magnetic plastic cards for rail tickets as far back as 1979, when it started the mass transit system. And the card has since been the model for other cities to adopt similar systems, such as London's Oyster card. But for Hong Kong, RFID and smartcard payments happened to come at a time when the city was ready to go more cashless. There had been a coin shortage in the late '90s and the result was a rapid adoption of Octopus for other payment situations such as supermarkets, parking lots, street parking meters, fast-food restaurants, and vending machines where consumers were making small payments.[19] The setup is such that Octopus can be embedded in a variety of objects, for example, a Hello Kitty ornament, an actual item sold on their site.

This wide adoption and variety of uses created a trend in Asia where consumers have long been comfortable paying with something other than cash. It also put consumers onto the notion of their identity being connected to something other than a physical card.

Contactless verification is also the same technology we use in our car key fobs when we simply hit a button. In other words, this tech exists in many other verticals besides clothing. Cost coming down, though, means that we can do more with RFID, with less concern about the cost of losing or disposing of individual chips. Paying twenty dollars for a new E-ZPass is onerous, but tossing out a shirt with a fifty-cent chip is not.

The fact is that we do want our clothes to do more. From a very basic level, there are simple extras, such as SCOTTeVEST, a clothing line that has multiple pockets, or Norma Kamali's iconic sleeping bag coat (does what the package says; coat doubles as a sleeping bag) that appeal because we have always wanted more function from our garments. Carolina Herrera has famously said she loves a dress with pockets. Clothing with utilitarian functions have longer shelf lives in our closets than items that are purely decorative. Consider the trench coat, or boat shoes that drain water, or diving watches that are effectively computers that monitor oxygen tank levels.

We love when our clothing can make our lives easier. Recently I was pitched a popular line of headsets called Wraps, whose headphones double as bracelets. As we saw in chapter 3, we love it if our bracelets also track our heartbeat or tell us about incoming text notifications. Google and Levi's have announced a connected jacket, using a conductive yarn called Jacquard, that will allow you to manage basic features of your smartphone such as playing music or answering the phone.[20] There are now countless bag brands that also charge your phone via portable batteries, including ones offered by Kate Spade. It may be the lure of having to carry less in an increasingly mobile world.

However, there was an actual moment when assistive clothing took a sharp left toward technology.

Utility took that distinct turn after September 11, 2001, in New York. General paranoia set in in many industries after the terrorist events of 9/11, but very heavily with clothing makers. While designers had been experimenting with environmentally protective garments for some time (such as UV-protective tops and pants), September 11 and then the 2005 London train bombings galvanized the fashion industry.

Pockets just stopped being enough. In the years after, Haspel created acid rain–proof men's suits and Hussein Chalayan took the sleeping bag one step further and made full-blown cocoon clothing. Bless inflated coats to Michelin Man–sized garments. Protective-gear company Damascus, which makes puncture-proof materials for riot/crowd control situations, and D3O (from the founder of North Face), which makes bulletproof flexible materials—think police forces' defensive clothing—both discovered that even regular customers want to buy their technical fabrics. Designers became or have since become obsessed with saving the world via garments, as people just couldn't feel safe enough. Or prepared enough. Designer Rhus Ovata went so far as to say that it was "the smell of blood in the air from another bomb exploding in Tel Aviv [that helped him] stay creative and passionate."[21]

The notion of using technology previously aligned for sportspeople (think chest mesh for fencers or pierce-proof elbow pads for motorsports), moved into the mainstream. Better safe than sorry. People's psyches turned in the direction of preparedness. If you open any outdoor-clothing catalog today, you will find more clothing with protective elements than ever before. And not just trench coats. The rush to bionic fabrics and bulletproof materials is now pervasive in everything from our workout gear to our suiting, whether we know it or not. It is reflective of how we as a society coped with a post-9/11 world, but also of a promise that you can be kept safe.

Taking my example from earlier about avalanches, one might ask the question of what might have happened in the days after 9/11 if RFID technology had been employed in all the clothing of the rescue workers or even in the suits of the employees who worked in the twin towers.

I am aware that this is a controversial thing to suggest. But keep in mind that in 2001, RFID was not yet in use the way it is becoming now. We simply did not have access that we have or will have in more recent times. If we remain true to the purpose of this book, we must use the past to think about our future and what we might be able to do going forward. Keep in mind that RFID can send multiple signals at a time, can transmit two-way messages, and in the last decade, tags have become inexpensive and small. What happens if we make this technology as ubiquitous as laptops and cell phones (two technologies once considered not portable)? Could we indeed save thousands of lives in every natural (or unnatural) disaster from here on?

If we start to think about the potentials of embedding RFID in clothing, it isn't only about terrorism or disaster, however. It is also about day-to-day utility.

About 60 percent of those suffering from Alzheimer's or dementia are prone to wandering.[22] About 93 percent of those found within twelve hours will survive; but 7 percent do not. So about one in fourteen don't make it. And of those gone for more than twenty-four hours, only a third survive.[23] According to the US Department of Health and Human Services, by 2040 21.7 percent of the population will be sixty-five or older, and by 2060, there will be 98 million elderly people. That's more than twice the number of older persons in 2014.[24] Considering that dementia is a disease that disproportionately strikes the elderly, as our population ages, embedding clothing with RFID might be a way to increase wanderers' survival rates.

Let's consider some other non-clothing-protection scenarios that are part of our future, and with each one, I'll bring you back to the connection of clothing and technology with some possibilities that you may not have thought of.

Most likely you have heard of driverless cars by now. Back when *Minority Report* came out, the idea of everyone floating along hands-free was a visual trick in a movie, but even back then, this was not a concept that only existed in a science fiction film. Driverless cars are called *autonomous vehicles* by the automotive industry, and the first example of this actually appeared in the 1980s, at Carnegie Mellon's Navlab and Mercedes-Benz and Bundeswehr University's Prometheus Project in 1987.[25] The idea is very simple. Robots don't make the mistakes that human beings do. They can better detect changes in the environment, such as another oncoming car or slick road conditions, and they also don't get tired after driving for long periods of time.

The human eye can see stars that are quite far away; however, our visual acuity and reflexes on the road are another matter. According to highway safety expert Marc Green, it takes us a long time to react to a pedestrian in the road. We don't only need to see; we need to detect, then also absorb, process, and decide. If a driver is traveling sixty miles per hour, the normal reaction time is 1.5 seconds, during which time the car will have moved 132 feet. But cars don't immediately come to a dead stop, which means that after the 1.5 seconds it takes to get around to applying the brake, there is another 3.4 seconds during which the car is traveling another 150 feet. Which means that in order to stop for a pedestrian in the road, we need a full 280 feet and 4.9 seconds. In city driving conditions, going at thirty-five miles per hour, you would need 138 feet and 3.6 seconds.[26] In New York City, by the way, that's half a city block.[27]

And that is assuming the car is not a tractor trailer; the road is not wet; the street does not slope downhill, and, oh by the way, the driver is not slowed down by age, alcohol, drugs, exhaustion, or any distractions, such as checking a cell phone!

Take the human factor out of the equation, and in theory, accidents should go down and collision avoidance rates should improve. Cars that can brake for you and park for you are already on the road. Parking assist is quite simple; it uses magnetic technology to send a signal to detect distance. The feedback is sent to the car's system which then adjusts.

However, there has been a lot written about driverless cars and all their related issues. There is, for example, the concern from the insurance industry as to who is liable in an accident if the driver is not actively driving. There are other concerns, such as whether autonomous cars can choose between saving the life of passengers in the car or pedestrians on the road. Recently there's been talk of whether car manufacturers have adequately hack-proof systems to withstand any attempts to weaponize vehicles. Without getting too far into ethics, for the purpose of this book, I want you to consider the possibilities of driverless cars as they apply to soft goods.

And if the soft-goods world can present a solution to some of these dilemmas, great.

What if we could use wearables to improve upon Green's statistics?

In 2008, a company called SmartCap came out with a baseball hat to detect truck drivers' EEG (electroencephalography) levels, essentially measuring whether a commercial vehicle driver's fatigue was hitting alarming levels.[28] The cap then uses Bluetooth technology to communicate a driver's exhaustion to a dashboard.

But what if we could take it even further?

Think of a gyroscope, a spinning disc that uses an axis to detect motion and maintain orientation. It is used in many navigation systems where magnetic compasses don't work or wouldn't be precise enough, such as ballistic missiles, telescopes, airplanes, or the Space Shuttle.[29] The smallest one is a fraction of the width of human hair.[30] Essentially any sudden motion or tilt would be detected.

So we might create an earring or an over-the-ear wearable—something like the hands-free headset—that contains a gyroscope. In the case of a drowsy driver, an autonomous vehicle would not need to rely solely on sudden lane drift; rather, the gyroscope would detect a sudden droop of the face or forward tilt of the head and, when combined with an RFID communication, could alert a computer inside the car to react in compensation for the driver and to either nudge the driver, say, with a small vibration, or step in to navigate and drive.

We might use eyeglass technology to read the blink or vision patterns of the wearer to predict and anticipate a driver's next actions. Does the driver see the pedestrian? In fog, we can only see a handful of feet in front of us, but computers can see much farther. Companies such as Cortexica are re-creating the human vision experience in technology.[31] And at MIT, teen genius Saumil Bandyopadhyay has created an infrared detector that allows vehicles to sense each other in fog or darkness. It is a breakthrough because, unlike previous technologies, Bandyopadhyay's invention is a nanotechnology that is not just tiny but functions at room temperature without the liquid nitrogen tanks normally required for infrared sensing.[32] Automakers want to embed this into cars such that they can react to each other. But what if we were able to embed that detector into a wearable eyeglass?

The device would come with you to each and every vehicle you might pilot, even, say, a rental car. Most insurance policies insure the driver, not the vehicle, and provided you are wearing the device, your improved vision would improve your insurance policy.

Let's take another wearable item that might provide basic protection: freedom from being mugged. If, in recent years, you bought a Samsung device that comes with a pen, then you know that the S Pen comes with a technology that detects when you are about to leave it behind. The pen alerts the device when the two items are drifting too far apart, and sends a signal that can then be picked up by whoever is carrying the device to go back and retrieve the stray pen. Eventually the use of styluses may become obsolete, go the way of other gadgets such as the pager, but the utility is the thought.

What if your bag or wallet came with similar technology?[33] Imagine the next time you are out for dinner. Either you take your wallet out and leave it on the counter or you've hung your bag under the table or behind you on a chair. Suddenly, you walk away to take a phone call and/or a petty thief comes through the restaurant. One way or another, you and your valuables are separated. What if a tiny GPS device in your bag alerted your phone? Your phone already has GPS technology and alert capabilities. Better yet, what if those alerts caused your wallet to yell out, "I'm being stolen!" or snapped a photo of the offender and texted it to your phone. If you've ever used "Locate My Phone" for an iPhone, then you've already used this technology, just not exactly the way I'm outlining it.

RFID and GPS both have their uses. RFID is inexpensive and localized. GPS, or global positions system, offers worldwide tracking. It currently relies on (as the acronym says) the global positioning of the twenty-four satellites in the sky above us. It also uses radio waves to triangulate location and time, but sent out to and from satellite systems as opposed to via ground-scanning technology. Therefore GPS is fantastic for anything we need to track that might be tens or thousands of miles away. The downside of GPS is that it is battery-reliant. But hold the thought, because there may be a solution.

GPS is becoming less and less expensive. In 2007, Texas Instruments announced a five-dollar GPS chip, at the time revolutionary.[34] By 2013, a company called Retrievor was making a GPS disk that costs just $1.79 per month to track each device.[35] By 2015, companies such as Tile and TrackR offered similar GPS tags that one can attach to anything.[36] I've been giving talks about the future since 1998, and I have yet to give one where someone has shown me a wallet or purse using the exact tech entirely embedded. One can certainly slip a TrackR or other similar chip inside a sleeve, but if the idea caught on within the apparel industry, we could see life-changing advances, because we would not be reliant on consumers having to opt in to tracking.

We've talked a lot in previous chapters about the environment and the world we live in. If we decide to embrace technology, what if embedding soft goods with technology could help us with the environment? The technology I mentioned earlier is small enough that it could, for example, be embedded into the heel of a shoe.

In 2008, a Rotterdam-based company called Energy Floors took the very simple idea of turning our kinetic energy into power sources for other objects.[37] The moderately active person takes 7,500 steps a day. If you live eighty years and maintain that level, you will take 216,262,500 steps in your lifetime.

That's 110,000 miles. Even half that would be a significant amount of energy generated.[38]

Energy Floors decided to create dance floors that would harness human footsteps and action and convert them into electricity. They were able to make an eco–dance club called Club WATT that generated 8 billion joules of electricity. CEO Michel Smit later told TED, the technology conference company, that the business model wasn't quite sustainable.[39] Just yet.

But no matter, the idea was there.

In 2009, Laurence Kemball-Cook, a British industrial designer, created Pavegen to manufacture flooring tiles made from recycled tires and intended to capture footstep energy and convert it to electrical energy to light up streets, festivals, or hallways. It took him to January 2015 to gain traction, but the company is getting there. Pavegen has deals with Samsung and Harrods, has tiles in Heathrow, and has tiled a Rio soccer pitch.[40] At the time of this book, there is one major obstacle: cost. It currently costs Pavegen £1,250 to cover one square meter of ground. From a business-model standpoint as well as an energy savings standpoint, it would take a while for a city or company to recoup that investment.

However, let's remember that ten years ago, technology costs were much higher also for RFID, GPS, and even solar panels.

Kemball-Cook is not the only one to be looking for ways for us to be our own power source. The University of Bolton's Institute for Materials Research and Innovation is working on a "photovoltaic-piezoelectric" flexible fiber to capture footsteps to power our devices.[41] Essentially, carpets that charge your phone.

All of this of course only works when you are on top of the surface. So how about this? What if we were able to harness that energy and put it into the heel of your shoe?

The challenge for us as a society has been that we think of fashion and we think of technology. But we do not think of them together. As I mentioned earlier, when we think of clothing, we think of *The Devil Wears Prada* and polka dots. And technologists rarely consider how we might make start innovation from the wearable standpoint over the delivery standpoint. We need to start thinking of the two together.

After all, clothing is your one environment that goes wherever you go.

In this example, tiles and flooring will not go with us everywhere. Is it possible to tile the entire world? It is a fantastic concept, but it is similar to having to seek out an electrical wall outlet when we need a power source.

Since about 2010, I have been suggesting that we take some of this microtechnology and implant it in items we can wear all the time, such as our shoes. If this technology came inside each pair of shoes, you would always be your own spare battery for your telephone.

Remember my thought earlier about the challenges of GPS requiring battery power? In 2013, a company called EPGL Medical created a micron-sized piezoelectric energy harvester for contact lenses by gathering energy from blinking and other eye movements to create a perpetual source of power for wearable displays.[42] While the company's website is mostly about augmented reality, offering virtual reality scenarios such as virtual workout environments and armchair travel experiences, digitized contact lenses would link many of the scenarios I suggest above.

Consider if those lenses had RFID or GPS as well. Thankfully, GPS chips have been coming down in size, which has been the primary obstacle to them being embedded in the highest-usability ways. In order for developers to truly add features, the chips need to be very small to gain widespread usage. At 10 by 10 by 5.8 millimeters and weighing 2.5 grams, microchips produced by Israeli-based OriginGPS now have integrated antenna and radio frequency shields.[43] And they continue to get smaller. And RFID is already there.

In a mining accident, first responders might see what buried miners are seeing if those miners were wearing augmented contact lenses. Rescue workers might also be able to detect the blood sugar levels or other health indicators of the wearers.

In driving situations, GPS systems might be able to constantly feed back road conditions or weather updates or even emergency occurrences such as live information on traffic accidents. Companies like Waze already have the technology to ascertain potential traffic chokepoints, but what if it could be taken one step further to, say, alert car accident rescue teams to the precise health requirements of victims? Smart lenses might be able to communicate information not just to the wearer but to outside sources, such as vehicles or family members.

At any given time, there will always be a technology "new new thing" that is either taking off or failing or simply changing, be it Google Glass or Snapchat Glasses. The actual fad is not what is important. Technology moves pretty quickly, so the point here is less to identify something that may exist ten years into the future, but to point out the connection and capability between technology and clothing. If we decide we don't want to live on the grid, we can harness existing technology and make our clothing work just a little bit harder on our behalves.

There has been much talk about the connected home. Journalists love to call this the Internet of Things.[44] This is where your various furniture, appliances, and fixtures, such as lighting, thermostat, and garage, are digitally managed through apps you might have on your cell phone, tablet, or laptop. At a very basic level, the promise of smart appliances offers a convenience that we didn't previously have. For example, say you go on vacation and forget to lock your doors, turn off lights, set your burglar alarm, or turn down your thermostat; now remote access to your fixtures allows you to do this from anywhere in the world.

But the idea of a connected home offers another promise when linked with soft goods and wearables. In 2003, the German supermarket company Metro Group opened the Extra Future Store market in Duisberg, Germany. Using Intel Corporation chips and Philips Semiconductor Code to process and track RFID chips, the idea was to show that a full connected supermarket could run much more efficiently than a traditional market. Using chip technology, the company could track inventory and expiration dates, as well as mitigate theft.[45] Say you pick up a carton of ice cream but decide against it on the way to the register and leave it in the bread aisle. Before it melts, a supermarket employee will be alerted as to where it is. When something is sold, inventory management systems will be alerted to reorder.

"Shrinkage" is an enormous cost for retailers. The Food Marketing Institute and The Retail Control Group's 2013 research study into loss indicates that 64 percent of store shrink is caused by poor store operations, with the other portion, 36 percent, caused by theft.[46] With technology, market managers would know when a piece of merchandise is nearing its expiration date and needs to be put on sale or whether it is walking out the door without having been scanned at the register.

How often have you gone to the market and forgotten to buy eggs? Or perhaps you checked your milk, and it was expired? Imagine now the connection of your home and your supermarket to your wearables.

Suppose the connected contact lenses I told you about have the capability to scan your refrigerator the moment you look inside. Guess what: You have three eggs left and, based on how often you like to eat eggs (your lenses, by the way, can gauge time), the lenses have told your supermarket to send you a new batch. In fact, your supermarket order is generated based on what remains in your refrigerator, what you like to eat, and when your food is about to expire. Have plans to travel? Your travel itinerary has been fed into your lenses, so no groceries will be ordered during the two weeks you're away from home.

When I address academic or corporate audiences, at this point at least some portion of the audience gets very nervous. "Privacy!" they yell. The notion of privacy is one that comes up in almost every discussion of technology and potential advances, and of course privacy is no joke.

I like to say that the store of the *future* includes blacklisting, facial recognition, and predictive shopping, but the truth is that some of this already exists. In that story about Swatch for the *Financial Times*, I wrote about the robot trend, where designers' manifestations of robot-themed items such as those at Prada and Kid Robot foreshadowed their concerns for the role technology plays in tracking and predicting our consumption behaviors. When that article came out, the debate was still on about whether e-commerce was viable.

But things changed literally within the year. The following year, 2006, that same robot trend forecasted an increasing interest in merging shopping with technology. I subsequently covered how stores were investing in technology to blacklist shoppers based on their returns, through companies such as The Return Exchange.[47] The illusion of anonymity was fast being erased. Shoppers who believed they could buy and return with impunity were about to find out that computers remembered their every digital move. Today you might not blink twice when you're asked to scan your driver's license while making a return, but back then, consumers were still alarmed.

However, with the advent of online shopping, retailers truly began to know everything there is to know about you: what size you wear, what brands you like, exactly what hangs in your closet, how much you paid for it, and the exact date on which you bought it. Looking at social media today, it's certain that this is no longer news. Companies like RevTrax, Tag New Media, and Inmar pay attention to how you spend, if consumers themselves don't already advertise their behaviors on Instagram, Snapchat, Pinterest, Vine, Periscope, WhatsApp, Tumblr, Flickr, or, in Asia, Weixin, Feixin, Sina Weibo, QQ, or Kakao. And forget the now old-school Facebook; have I mentioned you can also broadcast your behaviors and consumption on Blippy, Foursquare, Swipely, Dopplr, Blab, Yik Yak, Ello, and Kleek? The chances are, unless you are vehemently opposed to surfing the web, someone knows what you like to buy. In fact, if you've ever sent your DNA to Ancestry.com or 23AndMe, others know even more about you than that.

In 1999, when I gave my very first talk about mobile technology, I described a scenario where you could walk past a pizza store or, say, a chic new bar, and a coupon would be broadcast to your device, using proximity technology. Whether or not you happen to glance at the bar's storefront, or how long you lingered on the coupon, might also be registered.[48]

This may terrify you but it is already here.

In 2012, Target "outed" a pregnant teen to her family when her father discovered that the analysis of the combination of her purchases meant that she was expecting. The company had used "big data" or shopping analysis and knew the girl was pregnant practically before she even did, and started sending the family coupons for diapers.[49] This is not as hard as behavioral scientists would have you think. For example, a woman has suddenly stopped buying feminine protection because she has stopped menstruating. And at the same time, she's routinely nauseous so suddenly she starts buying antinausea medication. Perhaps it is even more subtle; she's suddenly gained a couple of pounds, so the size of her pants has changed. Or, as some pregnant women have experienced, her sense of smell changes, so suddenly she can't stand perfumed soaps and lotions, and she switches to unscented products.

It gets even more technical than just making a laundry list of what you've bought. Using military-grade facial recognition software, companies can employ technology to anticipate your every desire. Welcome to the *Minority Report* of shopping. By 2013, Virgin Mobile, Volkswagen, Nike, had all tried it. British charity Plan UK tested an ad on Oxford Street that only displayed if a woman was in front of it.[50] In January 2016, the BBC started testing if their native advertising was working for clients with facial reaction technology using the camera in your laptop.[51] Certainly people are still concerned. There is talk about more data privacy laws if this becomes used widely.[52]

But creeping consumers out is one thing; the ability of sites to tell you what you want, instead of you telling them, is already here. Although we are still learning how companies may use your information, the truth is they may not tell you everything. Is it a trade-off you're willing to make? It may be too late to back away. This promise of connectedness—or its implications—is already on its way to you.

In the 1987 film *Innerspace*, Dennis Quaid plays a miniaturized aviator who is injected into Martin Short's body.[53] As such, Quaid reports back on what's happening inside Short's body. Well, this technology exists today. It is called *edible computing*. A significant amount of the cost of a hospital stay today comes down to the occupation of a hospital bed. Now imagine if after an operation, that bed were freed up, because doctors could monitor you remotely—via, say, a computer chip you ate. The problem is the digestive tract will eventually pass the device.

How about a tattoo? Especially now that tattoos are not so uncommon. Companies such as Chaotic Moon have gone so far as to make temporary tattoos using electroconductive ink with sensors and trackers.[54] Turning you into a walking smart device. Going one step further, some people are willing to be microchipped. Tim Shank and Krissy Heishman are two people who have NFC subdermal chips that allow their hands to function as a key card.[55] It is possible that this will be the future, but edible and dermal devices, much less surgery, have their challenges: cost, communication, safety, and regulatory issues.

They're possible, but let's tackle something billions of people on the planet already have.

The Apple watch was launched in 2013.[56] It was not the first smart watch, far from it. The first attempt at a smart watch was in 1983, when Seiko came out with the Data 2000. It was really Bill Geiser who, with a company called Three-Five Systems, in partnership with Fossil Watches, made a screen small enough to work with Palm Pilot's systems in 2002 and got the trend going. Not only did it run a wide range of programs, but it connected to a desktop to save data.

In the last three years, however, there is much talk of the battle for the wrist. The wristwatch market is expected to reach $46 billion by the end of 2017. But it isn't because telling time has suddenly become en vogue, when we now can use our mobile phones to do so. It is because of the wearable market. When people ask me why I moved from writing about apparel for the weekend pages of the *Financial Times* to another section of the paper, the "Watches and Jewellery Report," I say it's because as a futurist, I headed to the next logical frontier.

Coming somewhat full circle in this chapter, in January 2016, I wrote about Swatch and Visa's partnership[57] as sponsors for the 2016 Summer Olympics. The October prior, Swatch had released, with China's Bank of Communications and the China UnionPay network, the Swatch Bellamy watch, which allows the wearer to make contactless purchases using electromagnetic near-field communication (NFC) technology instead of RFID. The Bellamy is named for American author Edward Bellamy, whose 1888 science fiction novel, *Looking Backward: 2000-1887*, described a socialist, cashless society where wealth is distributed to citizens via debit cards. A month later, Swatch announced a separate partnership with Visa, and, in early 2016, came out in the United States, Brazil, and Switzerland with a Bellamy version capable of accepting worldwide payments.

The reason this was interesting to me has nothing to do with the brand—it didn't need to be Swatch per se. What I found interesting was that it pitted a ninety-dollar watch against companies that have come out with mobile wallets for our phones, such as Apple Pay, Android Pay, and Samsung Pay, meaning that it was affordable to a much broader population than, say, a $600 smartphone. Granted, ninety dollars may not be an impressively low number—yet. But remember that RFID, GPS, and NFC are all becoming less and less expensive every day.

It also doesn't require the satellite systems that cell phone companies do, making Swatch and Visa a potential payment competitor in areas of the world where cell phone technology may be spotty or communities have lower levels of access to technology.

Places such as India and Kenya.[58]

The Indian subcontinent has a history of earthquakes.

In 2015 alone, there were seven. The one on April 25, 2015, killed more than 8,900 people. A decade earlier, the one on October 8, 2005, killed 130,000 people. And the one a year earlier, December 26, 2004, that I mentioned at the beginning of this chapter took the lives of 15,000 in India.[59]

Consider with me what might have happened if even a fraction of those people just happened to have a GPS or NFC wearable on their wrist.

BURKINIS AND THE
CLASH OF CIVILIZATIONS

W E'VE LOOKED at when to pay attention to movements
and shifts in clothing, how to use clothing to spot the lies
we are telling ourselves, some past predictions, and our
daily and group futures. But clothing doesn't only reflect or forecast your
personal safety or shifting economies; it also tells you about the greater
world in which all these things lie. Clothing in fact reflects the clash of
civilizations.

After the terror attacks of September 11, 2001, it was a challenge
for travelers to simply get onto a plane. Only three ounces of liquid!
Bag charges! No carry-ons![1] To this day, I argue, who can keep up with
the ever-changing regulations of the TSA? Small knives but no liquids?[2]
Even if one diligently attempts to follow the regs, they change from airport to airport, from carrier to carrier.[3]

This wasn't just about the issue of danger symbols or dangerous jewelry we talked about in chapter 1; designers actually responded by making changes in the clothing they were providing to us. Many of them
started to make convertible clothing: pants that become a dress or a top
that becomes a bag. Or better yet, a coat that becomes a tote that also
becomes a sleeping bag. The sudden obsession with one piece for all uses

was a reflection of how it had become more complicated to travel than ever before.

Making things worse were news items such as the fact that when the TSA took over air safety in 2002, it added twenty thousand workers, many of whom were hired without background reviews—and a significant number of them had felony criminal records.[4] Which meant that at once travelers feared their goods would be stolen when checked. And also that clearing security often meant a wide variety of interpretations.[5]

Certainly, designers were ready for this widespread feeling of DIY doomsday prepper. They reacted by creating those hybrid clothes not just for paranoid or elite travelers, but so all of us wouldn't need to check bags. Norma Kamali went so far as to sell the sleeping-bag coat I mentioned earlier—at Walmart.[6]

But there was more reflected in it than utilitarian concerns. Because let's be real, how often are you really going to need your coat to become a bed?[7]

Rather, it was more a sense of the earth shifting below us. The world around us quite literally changing. Migrating. Moving. Uncertain.

You never know what might come next.

It was feeling as though you never know when you might need shelter on the go—even if you never do. The link between terrorism, travel, and clothing is one that is not just about convenience. The restrictions reflect the fact that culture is our new war. The fact that many, many people, not just some niche cluster, felt this way, was telling.

In the summer of 1993, Samuel P. Huntington published a paper aptly named "The Clash of Civilizations?" in the journal *Foreign Affairs*.[8] In it, he postulated that our future conflicts with each other would be cultural and not solely financial or political. He could not have been more right. In his essay, Huntington indicated that rivalries between countries would not be simply around borders, but around the belief systems that are held by Western, Confucian, Japanese, Hindu, Islamic, Slavic Orthodox, Latin American, and African civilizations. That essentially, if we are divided into these groups, we hold not just differing concepts of history, tradition, and language, but also inescapably different notions of religion, views of ourselves versus the state, views of family, and what we consider to be our fundamental rights and place in society. Our feelings about who we are in relationship to our parents, our significant others, and our children, as well as our notions of equality, authority, and liberty are all wrapped up in the product of centuries. And moreover, they are hard to change.

Now I am simplifying Huntington quite a bit—his essay became a book—but what he was really saying is that these fundamental concepts stay with us as individuals longer than any government in power might. In other words, toppling governments or long, drawn-out wars, cannot easily unseat these personal beliefs.

If this is the case, and we think about how we see culture, clearly one way we see culture immediately is in clothing. A study done in 2011 called "Looking the Part: Social Status Cues Shape Race Perception," showed that simply by looking at an outfit, we derive ideas of race and class, without ever seeing a person's skin tone or face.[9] That is, clothing can message our culture and which civilization we ascribe to all by itself, without a single other identifying factor.

Huntington of course wrote his essay before the Internet evolved into the way we know it today. However, the world is now smaller due to the Internet. We have the ability to see what people are wearing around the world.

By 2012 or 2013, the personal-style blogger became a financial force to be reckoned with.[10] The reason was that the Internet made it so that millions could have access to one person's clothing messaging. To view, to emulate, to criticize, to purchase. Chiara Ferragni, the personality behind the blog *The Blonde Salad*, reportedly made in excess of $8 million in 2014.[11] Companies such as LIKEtoKNOW.it, Have2Haveit, and ShopStyle have been created and now have revenue streams propped up entirely on the shoulders of social media communicating what clothing we should be wearing.[12] They don't have stores, they don't rely on magazines, and they only need one social post to sell out an item.

It can be argued that the Kardashians' $300 million fortune would not exist were it not for social media.[13] They had a television show, but that television show only reached an estimated 1.4 million people.[14] Were it not for their combined Instagram account reach of three hundred million, would they be known on the other side of the world?[15]

In essence, anyone with access to the Internet now has access to fashion or, rather, notions of culture.

In other words:

Culture is the new war →
How do we see culture? →
We see culture in clothes →
The world is smaller due to the Internet →
Clothes are communicated on the Internet via social media →
Culture from other parts of the world, or more importantly, other
    civilizations are at our fingertips every day, unavoidable.

Huntington wrote that the fact that Northern Africans were emi-grating to Europe was causing hostility. Where once the West was viewed as the epicenter of refinement and elites of the West viewed themselves as the only developed peoples, this shift caused an Us versus Them.

Indeed, in the summer of 2009, French swimming pools banned the *burkini*, a one-piece swim costume created by Muslim designers for women who wanted to go swimming yet remain covered.[16] Then on April 23, 2010, a French woman wearing an Islamic face veil was fined by the French police in Nantes,[17] as France's president Sarkozy pushed to outlaw burqas and niqabs nationwide.[18] Then the French lower house of Parliament overwhelmingly approved a ban on wearing face-covering veils in a public place and with little to no government opposition; on April 11, 2011, the ban took effect.[19]

This meant that suddenly women could go topless in Cannes but not wear veils anywhere in France. The move in France, which has Western Europe's largest Muslim population, estimated to be at least five million, immediately worried Muslims in the Arab world and angered Muslims in Europe, to the point where France's Parliamentary Majority leader Jean-Francois Cope, who was behind the movement, had to be given police protection.[20] The day the ban took effect, arrests were made.[21]

All this was before the French elections, a response to this far-right clash to a large extent. But France was not alone. In April 2010, Bel-gium's lower house of Parliament passed a ban, leaving only a Senate vote to turn it into law. In June 2010 the Spanish Senate approved a motion urging Prime Minister Zapatero to also ban full-body veils.[22] With approximately 1.57 billion Muslims in the world, Islam is the sec-ond-largest religion and the fastest growing.[23] This ban literally repre-sented the clash of civilizations.

When I first started keeping an eye on the burkini problem, it was a blip in a newspaper, buried deep, with some humor. Clothing is not always taken seriously. That was before the Arab Spring. At the time, I asked myself, *What implications does this have for fundamentalists and terrorist movements? Does this really have to do with an item of clothing?* It does.

There are a number of issues all around this one item of clothing. Let's start with the issue in France and why it matters, and then I will bring it back to the United States and what all this means for us. Then we'll look at some questions for other parts of the world.

When France passed the first ban in 2010, it was done with the reasoning that anything that hides the face in public might be an issue of public safety. In other words, if you commit a crime, how could national security measures such as closed-circuit television correctly identify you if your face is hidden? On the face of it, it wasn't illogical; it just didn't apply to any other clothing item that might hide the face. For example, laws against overly large brimmed hats or giant sunglasses or frosted motorcycle helmets don't exist. The law unequally applies to the full-face veil, the niqab, which only leaves the eyes exposed. [24]

But by 2016, the illusion of the ban as a public safety measure had long been discarded. The ban was out-and-out described as a response to a social threat to the French way of life. By the summer of 2016, more than thirty French towns had banned the so-called burkinis.[25] Were French beaches overrun with women in full burqas everywhere? Of course not.

Right-wing candidate Marine Le Pen of the National Front party said, "The French beaches are those of Bardot and Vadim. . . ." Le Pen was calling to mind France's 1950s and '60s actress and sex symbol Brigitte Bardot[26] and director Roger Vadim, her one-time husband, who himself was known for coupling up with numerous other women considered to be paragons of sex appeal, such as Catherine Deneuve and Jane Fonda (before she took up the flag for feminism).[27]

"And not those of Belphegor," referring to a demon who is Hell's ambassador to France in De Plancy's 1818 *Dictionnaire Infernal*. "France does not lock away a woman's body," continued Le Pen.[28]

My word, a missionary from Hell? Just for covering up?

But as various cities continued to ban the burkini, two things became apparent. First, some mayors enacting the ban, such as Mayor Olivier Majewicz of Oye-Plage and Mayor Daniel Fasquelle of Le Touquet, had never seen a burqa and could not even identify one.[29] Second, women who chose to wear a long-sleeved T-shirt and trousers on the beach were finding themselves targeted, according to Marwan Muhammad, the executive director of the Center Against Islamophobia. Muslim women who didn't want to spend the 40 to 125 euros for a burkini were simply wearing regular clothing. And being asked to disrobe.[30]

A long-sleeved T-shirt? Which one of us who has been to the beach has not occasionally been sunburned or worried about getting sunburned? Imagine being asked to leave the beach unless you took off your shirt? One certainly cannot argue that a T-shirt poses a threat to national security. What part of the body are we trying to prevent someone from identifying?

Was France's message "Come to our beaches, and show us your breasts"? "We have a right to see them!"?

I challenge you at this time to draw a burkini. If like me, you immediately gravitate to the "tank top attached to a long bike short" swimsuits that Victorian-era women wore in France, the United States, and England before the invention of the bikini, you would be wrong. It turned out that there was no legal definition of a burkini.[31] What exactly is one?

Nonetheless, by mid-August 2016, the burkini ban went into effect, and those found to be in violation were asked to leave or could be fined thirty-eight euros—or they could strip. On August 25, the image of a woman sitting on the ground in Nice, France, surrounded by four men with A4 assault rifles as they forced her to take off her clothes, hit the front pages of many national newspapers.[32] It wasn't even a burkini; it was a regular shirt.

The French cited *laïcité*, which can best be summed as "secularism in public." In other words, one should not display one's religious beliefs in any which way, shape, or form when out and about. In schools, malls, hospitals, and other public arenas of life, it is considered culturally wrong to display artifacts or identifications of religion.[33]

But one would be hard-pressed to find similar clashes or conflicts or public outcry over the French wearing, say, a cross or a Jewish star necklace, or affixing a mezuzah, the encasement of a piece of parchment containing verses from the Torah, to some Jewish businesses or households.[34] Scholars would argue that the burkini ban's interpretation of secularist ideology is bastardized, not to mention convenient and selective.

The reality, I would also argue, is that the burkini, or one's long-sleeved T-shirt stand-in, reflects the culmination of fear around terrorism.

We remember that after 9/11, traveling with danger symbols turned into—and remains—a worldwide problem. In fact, my brother told me that he had a terse conversation with Chinese security at the Beijing airport (in August 2016) when he happened to have on hand a gift for me, a plastic purse shaped as two emojis, the unfortunate choice of a cartoon bomb and the yellow explosion star.

Well, the burkini enforcement is not coincidentally timed. France had just come off a series of terrorist attacks that rocked the country.

On January 7, 2015, two assailants shot up the offices of satirical newspaper *Charlie Hebdo*, killing twelve people.[35] Then two days later, at the Porte de Vincennes, another person claiming allegiance to the Islamic State took hostages and killed another five people.[36] But on November 13, 2015, five coordinated attacks at the Stade de France, Saint-Denis, followed by an attack on the Bataclan, killed 137 people and injured another 368.[37] During Bastille Day, France's Independence Day, July 14, 2016, a Tunisian resident of France drove into the crowds in Nice, France, killing 87 and hurting 434.

When attacks of this nature occur, journalists often argue about the term *terrorist*. Is it terrorism if it is a sole actor or group of actors who may or may not have any connection to known terrorist groups? Is it an act of terrorism but not necessarily by a terrorist? It has remained unclear whether Lahouaiej-Bouhlel, the Nice attacker, was linked to terrorist groups.[38] In many recent rampages in the United States, such as the December 2015 San Bernardino attack and the June 2016 Orlando nightclub attack, the perpetrators are American citizens.[39]

Which begs the question, how does the layperson identify a threat? We know of course that national and international security services keep databases, but how does the everyday passerby assess whether a given person shares the same cultural viewpoints or notions toward the state and its civilians that he or she does?

Do we fall back on, as the study cited earlier suggests, clothing as the one distinguishable banner of who is and who is not a threat?

French Socialist prime minister Manuel Valls certainly thinks so. He called the burkini "an affirmation of political Islam." In other words, not just a religious symbol, but actually fighting words. A statement of imminent risk and one imbued with all the messages intended in a clashing.[40] Wow.

Let's set aside our emotions for the moment.

If we remember that math doesn't lie, then we can look at this risk utilizing pure data. Consider the following death rates:

Death by the LA gangs Crips and Bloods:[41] 15,000[42]
Fatal drunk driving: 9,967[43]
Accidental drowning typically in backyard pools: 3,536[44]
ISIS: 1,200[45]

It is obviously important to note that these are over varying time points: The LA gangs have been active over forty years: the drowning data are from a ten-year time frame. Unfortunately, the drunk-driving figure is just for one year in the United States. To clarify further, the 150,000 to 200,000 killed in Iraq since 2003 have been related to domestic conflict alone and the 400,000 in Syria's civil war predominantly a result of Assad's military bombing of cities.[46] In other words, from a pure data standpoint, the threat we perceive from ISIS is not proportional to the reaction.

Now of course that could change in the future. And—giant disclaimer here—I am not trying to convince you that ISIS is not a threat. It's clearly a huge problem.

But there is a reason why the image of the woman being forced to take off her T-shirt on a French beach is so right to France and so wrong in the eyes of the rest of the world. In other words, our perception of conflict and the clash between civilizations is not necessarily proportional to the data. You are much less likely to die from ISIS than at the hands of a drunk driver. The threat felt in France is not one of actual "death by ISIS"; rather, it is a threat of cultural erosion. Our taxonomy of fear is changing, and we are seeing this play out in clothing.

This is similar to the way society reacts to child molestation. We now know that a child is more likely to be harmed by someone he or she knows, either a family member or an acquaintance. Only approximately 10 percent of perpetrators of child sexual abuse are strangers.[47] Yet we still spend an inordinate amount of budget on educating children about "stranger danger." For example, a nationwide program that began in 2012 called "Tricky People" was covered by the *Today Show*, CBS, and even CBC, a Canadian channel, as it is currently in the process of being rolled out to American schools.[48] Should we educate children about strangers? Of course, but why do we focus on strangers instead of familial threats? We do so because we are uncomfortable with the thought that it is in our own families. It can be argued that kids today are not as free to play as thirty years ago. And that this is largely due to the perception of, not the actual, danger to them.

Similarly the threat of the burkini is not about actual physical threat, it is about the encroaching Muslimization of the West and a tiredness that Europe feels with putting up with other cultures. This exhaustion is perfectly captured in Michel Houllebecq's book *Submission*, which was published just hours before *Charlie Hebdo* was attacked, in which Houllebecq fictionalized a near-future France with an Islamic Prime Minister.[49] While some considered the book wildly Islamophobic and offensive, its defenders said it was more about the corruption and venality of Europe itself that would permit such a takeover.[50]

"Submission" is, of course, the direct meaning of the word *Islam*, and I think it's really at the heart of what the West finds so threatening about the religion.[51] We are seeing to some extent clothing playing out in the work of political commentators such as Dinesh D'Souza and Norman Podhoretz, who have been writing for twenty years about the concept of Islamofascism, which they see as directly antithetical to democracy, individualism, and liberty.[52]

It is clothing as a symbol, and the banning of clothing is not about death on the battlefield; rather the battle is being fought through clothing. The battle is for our hearts and minds, and what we see, wear, and perceive is as important as actual human death. In this way, the issue of the burkini shows the power of clothing.

There is another reason I bring up the similarity between this and the way society has reacted to child molestation. There is something of a fear taking place around kids of the West being seduced and taken away by "radical Islam." Remember the cases of the three British schoolgirls running away to join ISIS?[53] There's something worrisome about losing one's kids. Replace the jeans that parents in the fifties hated as a symbol of rebellion, or the tattoos and piercings of later generations, with hijabs, and there you have it.

In the United States, all of this raises a whole other set of issues. Even if we will never go to France, we wonder how we ourselves would reconcile the matter. If we take away all of the other constructs around the burkini and leave it at *laïcité*, we see that the French may have no issue with their ban because of their secularism. But in the United States, we have a distinct separation of church and state. State cannot legislate our religious freedoms.

At the announcement of the French court's ruling, representing President Obama, White House spokesman Josh Earnest said that the United States did not want to "second-guess" France, but that Obama "believes strongly in the freedom of religion." Secretary General Ban Ki-moon's chief spokesman, Stéphane Dujarric, who had previously stated concern around the burkini ban, said at a news briefing, "Obviously we welcome the decision by the court" and emphasizing "the need for people's personal dignity to be respected."[54]

That freedom of religion has not stopped Islamic dress from being an issue in America, of course. We can see this easily in the rise in bullying of Muslims, in particular, kids. In Florida, a high school French teacher was reported to have called a fourteen-year-old student a "raghead Taliban." In Texas, an economics teacher sent students home with a study guide he created, titled, "Islam/Radical Islam (Did You Know?)" indicating what to do "if taken hostage by radical Islamists." Children report being called terrorists and having rocks thrown at them. A 2014 survey of California students found that 29 percent of those who had worn a hijab had experienced offensive touching or pulling of their head scarves.[55] Indeed there is evidence that certain articles of clothing are now identified as ISIS signifiers to other children.[56]

We are now seeing this fear play out in the United States. On January 27, 2017, President Trump enacted a travel ban against seven predominantly Muslim nations.[57] There's just one problem. Between 1975 and 2015, citizens from those countries killed exactly zero people in terrorist attacks on American soil.[58]

In general, the data between immigration and crime do not support this link. Alex Nowrasteh, an immigration expert at the Cato Institute, a libertarian think tank, conducted a study that showed that Americans are six times more likely to die from a shark attack, twenty-nine times more likely to die from an asteroid strike, and 6.9 million times more likely to die from cancer or heart disease, than being killed by an immigrant-turned-terrorist on US soil.[59] Apparently, my chances of winning the Powerball lottery are greater!

Yet as this clash plays out in America, leading to attacks on immigrants and kids being harassed in schools, it raises the question of whether it is safer for everyone if people are not allowed to wear them.[60]

Unlike Europe, this would lead to many lawsuits and become an issue for the American Civil Liberties Union, among others, around issues of religious freedom. After all, the reality is that hijabs have nothing to do with who is safe. Even the famous are not immune. Olympian Ibtihaj Muhammad, the American fencer, has reported being followed home and threatened because of her head scarf.[61]

But the issue of crossing borders—and what this kind of clothing tells us—is that we are looking at facing "border clashes" every single day.

This is not only true in Europe and in the United States.

The frontline of cultural clashes no longer exists in just a physical border but as nearby as the Internet. In July 2016, Pakistani social media star Qandeel Baloch was murdered by her brother in an alleged "honor killing" in the province of Punjab. The issue was her posting of photographs and videos of herself online, through which she became a household name and celebrity.[62] Then in September 2016, Saudi Arabian teen Abu Sin was jailed for flirting online with a twenty-one-year-old American YouTube star, Christina Crockett. Riyadhi authorities described the giggling and teasing as "unethical behavior," with police asking people to report similar occurrences in order to "preserve the values" of Saudi communities.[63]

In other words, technology and the rapidity of its advancement, has brought the clash of civilizations to our doorsteps—and to those in the Middle East as well. When Samuel P. Huntington wrote his original clash-of-civilizations essay, people were really only thinking about Islam coming to the West. However, as more and more people worldwide have access to social media, the clash that we are seeing play out in Europe is beginning to play out in other parts of the world as well. The arrest of someone flirting online or a Pakistani girl being killed for being in immodest clothing and projecting that globally have much to do with changing norms about female modesty as people normalize closer and closer to each other. What is also true about social media such as YouTube, SnapChat, and Instagram is that it also means that people can "out" others to the "modesty police."

The burkini is not the only clothing showing us this clash of civilizations. Asia too is changing very rapidly. Let's look at how India is dealing with shifting socially engineered constructs of appropriateness when it comes to their clothing.

With the popularity in the country of reality television, YouTube, and Bollywood, a whole generation is having much difficulty trying to figure out how to dress. Bollywood, the name given to the Hindi-language aspect of India's movie industry based in Mumbai, generated $4.5 billion in 2016, a figure that has grown from $3 billion since 2011, with gross receipts having tripled since 2004.[64] The films are incredibly popular in places as far away as Russia, Senegal, Nigeria, and Egypt, and have been cited as both influencing Baz Luhrmann to make *Moulin Rouge!* and fueling Western productions of musicals, namely, *Chicago, The Producers, Rent, Dreamgirls, Hairspray, Sweeney Todd, Across the Universe, The Phantom of the Opera, Enchanted,* and *Mamma Mia!*[65] Bollywood star Deepika Padukone is the world's tenth most highly paid actress; in other words, she is not just a nationwide role model, but an international one.[66] There are over 1.5 million Google results for her, and one category of her results is "Body": in other words, how Padukone looks and dresses as an icon. Clothing and its voice to the masses reach so much farther than we ever thought it would, as a result of technology.

Historically, Bollywood was known for skirting the line with sexualization—just showing midriff and maybe short shorts but never more than that, and very suggestive romance scenes but never actual kissing and definitely not sex—really very symbolic of the impossible demands placed on women in the modern media age: Be sexual but not too much. It wasn't until the 1990s that kissing was allowed on screen.[67] It had been banned beforehand and is still often frowned upon.[68]

Sarika Persaud, a New York City doctoral student of school and clinical psychology, wrote on her blog, *sword + flute,* in 2013, that the "modest Hindu woman" is struggling with concepts of how to appear modest, and not "distract men." She points to perceptions in Indian culture about whether or not women should cover up.[69]

All of this is coming at a time when attitudes toward women in India are in crisis.

In the Indian religious texts, women are considered "sinful, poison, living lies." Rape is glorified or deemed necessary in many of the country's myths about gods. Brihaspati rapes his pregnant sister-in-law, Mamata. Another Indian god, Vishnu, rapes Vrinda, and the act is justified because Vrinda's husband Shankachuda will be invincible in war unless her virtue is destroyed. In other words, the god Vishnu is considered a war hero for his act of violence.[70]

Today, real rape in India is at an all-time high.[71] Rape in India has skyrocketed from 24,206 reported rapes in 2011 to 37,000 in 2014.

Where just a handful of years ago that statistic was that every twenty-two minutes a woman in India is raped, it has now become as frequent as every fifteen minutes, and one is assaulted every two minutes.[72] The general lack of respect for women can be seen not just in the horrific attacks themselves, but in that offenders are released and repeat assaults on victims by the same perpetrators seem common.[73]

In December 2014, Bollywood actor Gauhar Khan was slapped by an audience member while taping a television show. The perpetrator who rushed onto the stage tried to touch the actor. When she resisted, he then slapped her, subsequently telling police officials the reason for his attack was that he objected to the actor dancing racily to "cheap songs," despite being a Muslim, and to her "skimpy outfits" and "short" dresses.[74]

Speaking of dancing, let us not dance around the issue.

The other reason the image of the Muslim woman on the beach surrounded by police made front pages was that it raised the question of patriarchy. Should men in power, such as Nicolas Sarkozy, Manuel Valls, Cannes mayor David Lisnard (the first to ban the burkini), or the heavily armed guards on the beaches, be dictating what a woman can and cannot wear? That, when asked, she must strip? That by law, he can force her to disrobe?

Lisnard has called the burkini "ostentatious dress."[75] In other words, some articles of clothing a woman wears are acceptable, but others are not. And that can be legislated.

Mayor Gil Bernardi of Le Lavandou has even called the idea of covering up on the beach "unhygienic."[76]

Huh?

Take a moment to Google the word "unhygienic" and "dress" and you'll find that unhygienic is a word associated with many traditional religions that consider menstruation "ritually unclean."[77] A cross-cultural study by anthropologists Thomas Buckley and Alma Gottlieb showed that menstruation is nearly universally considered taboo, dirty, and unhygienic.[78] The whole thing is wrapped up in men's ideas about women and their bodies.

If in recent years, you've ventured onto social channels and thought, *Why are there so many naked millennials?* this isn't in your imagination.[79] Half of all millennials admit that they have texted another person naked photos of themselves.[80] Even more eyebrow-raising is that according to a Mastercard survey, a full 62 percent of them would rather have their naked photos circulating on the web than have their financial data breached. The general population, in other words, older than thirty-five by the year 2015, is more modest, with only 55 percent willing to let strangers see them in the buff.[81]

One might object and say that the modern Instagram-y world is more free, but perhaps it is also more exploitative. There is a substantial amount currently being written about the rise of social media leading to image pressure for girls to disrobe, often unwillingly, probably the best-known being *Girls and Sex* by Peggy Orenstein and *American Girls* by Nancy Jo Sales.[82] In both books young girls report escalated levels of depression and suicidal thoughts over feeling the pressure to send nude photos of themselves.

Israel resident Nava Brief-Fried even made the news for launching her online store ModLi, a marketplace just dedicated to dressing modestly, when she decided that "today everything is so immodest."[83]

What matters is that it is totally asymmetric. There is little such increase in pressure for boys, in this or any other society.

Overwhelmingly women who wear the burkini, hijab, or burqa indicate that it is their choice to do so. The quotes by French officials in the media that the women are oppressed simply aren't true. Morgan Galawi, a woman born in Nice, said, "It's my choice to wear the headscarf."[84] A report by the *New York Times* in 2010 showed that American Muslim women who were covering up did so of their own choice, often citing the restriction as a way to be closer to Allah, or God, or a daily reminder of their faith.[85] Ibtihaj Muhammad, the Olympic fencer, made it clear at the SXSW festival that the garment was her choice when she objected to organizers' requests for her to remove her scarf.[86] Although medaling in Rio, she received undue attention for wearing her hijab. Her fencing was overshadowed by articles in *People*, the *Washington Post*, the *Atlantic*, *Us Weekly*, and *USA Today* that all focused on her clothing choices.[87] There is an assumption of oppression that does not appear to be borne out. At the 2016 Democratic National Convention, when Ghazala Khan, the mother of fallen soldier Humayun Khan, stood on stage wearing a head scarf, Donald Trump told the media that maybe she wasn't allowed to speak, expressing classic clothing-based Islamophobia.[88]

An ironic and sexist fact is that none of the attackers I cited who attacked France were burqa-wearers; they were all regular-looking men in regular dude clothes. The war of the burkini is a war fought between men of one civilization and men of another, neither of which cares what the other wears, but both wanting control over what their women wear, as a symbol of loyalty to them—like male animals fighting over a female harem. It is a debate in which women are the property and not the decision-makers.

Could we say that at its heart, this battle over clothing is actually one fought for control of all of these women: actress Gauhar Khan, the anonymous French beach woman, Ghazala Khan? On one side, millennial girls in the West feel increasing pressure to show themselves off against their will—the same as men using the Internet to assert control over women's bodies—a pressure to be hot. And even slutty, maybe? And in other parts of the world, such as India, is there a different yet similar difficulty for women as television and the web accelerate the pressure to be somewhat sexualized but "not too much," with violent consequences for thousands?

Why isn't this culture war being fought over men's clothes? Why do we fear the burqa if none of the actual terrorists wore one? Why don't millennial boys feel depression about pressure to send naked pics?

Regardless of whether someone embraces it or rejects it, it cannot be denied that norms about clothing are changing. And that overwhelmingly the power struggle around these clothing issues is around women's clothing. What all these women—Qandeel Baloch, Ghazala Khan, French hijab wearers, Ibtihaj Muhammad, millennial American girls, the Indian Bollywood star—have in common is that they all want or should have the right to choose for themselves what to wear, rather than to have it imposed on them as part of this culture war.

Nike has announced that they will make a Pro Hijab for Muslim athletes.[89] In 2016, Cagla Buyukakcay became the first Turkish woman to place in a French Open Grand Slam singles match.[90] Top ranked tennis player Aravane Rezaï is French Iranian and plays for France.[91] Both athletes are Muslim, and while neither player wears a hijab in competition, they are at the forefront of increasing numbers of female Muslim athletes on the pro stage. What will the French mayors do during the French Open if Nike's garment makes an appearance?

At the time of this writing, the mayors, some twenty-eight of them, are refusing to back down. The law has been overturned by France's highest court, but they are refusing to remove the burkini ban.[92] After all, at the heart of this ethical debate is their issue of identity. Not just France's, but their idea of what constitutes a woman's identity. Take note that there is no ban on how Islamic men dress on the beach. The clash of civilizations, whether real or perceived, is a war for power between men over women's bodies as a prize; clothes or a lack thereof are the weapons, and the Internet is simply a newer, bigger, faster battleground.

Clothing is so important that people are using the burkini to draw a line in the sand, an imaginary border. It is not just an instrument; it is also a weapon. It is a gun of this war.

CONCLUSION

The Power to Change Everything

THERE'S A scene from the movie *The Adjustment Bureau* (in which Matt Damon plays a puppet politician) where he says,

> This isn't even my tie. This tie was selected for me by a group of specialists in Tenafly, New Jersey, who chose it over fifty-six other ties we tested. In fact, our data suggested I have to stick to either a tie that is red or a tie that is blue. A yellow tie made it look as if I was taking my situation lightly and I may in fact pull my pants down again at any moment. A silver tie meant that I had forgotten my roots. My shoes . . . you know, shiny shoes we associate with high-price lawyers and bankers. If you want to get a working man's vote, you need to scuff up your shoes a little bit. But you can't scuff them up so much that you alienate the lawyers and bankers 'cause you need them to pay for the specialists back in Tenafly.[1]

Too much scruff equals clumsy. Not enough scruff equals lazy. A yellow tie, too flippant.

In other words, clothing is perception in politics. Clothing is manufactured in politics.

And of course, perception is everything.

It is about the manufacturing of image, one could say, such as with the Kardashians, but it is also that we reflect our political landscape and what seem to be unrelated issues—such as how much money we give to higher education—in our clothing.

We are in confusing times, where we are trying to figure out who we are and what our identity is, even as subcultures have risen to the forefront.

An article in the *New York Times* recently pronounced the return of the corset, that article of clothing interlacing the history of men and women (men wore them at one point as well), notions of freedom, work and gender roles, all into one.[2] At the same time even government agencies and airlines are struggling with ideas around dressing, covering up, and the illegality of passengers being asked to switch seats for religious reasons.[3]

As you've seen in the previous chapters, clothing has the ability to take the pulse of the world in any given moment, such as how we feel about demagogues or Bitcoin or living on Mars. These trends are reflecting how we deal with everything from natural disasters to environmental realities to terrorism to our fear of the end of the world—and they are part of how we are shaping the future.

How we handle both our physically shifting earth and our sociologically shifting world.

That clothing is a part of so many aspects of our daily lives, our messaging, our choices, our struggles, and our wars provides an unparalleled tool.

How you use that tool is up to you.

You could use it to think about what will happen in the next five years economically. Or what is happening with the person right next to you, that person's feelings, fears, and perhaps desires, even when they're false. Maybe it is just about buying the scarf that can protect you from an anthrax attack.

To think about clothing this way is not as hard as it would seem.

As I mentioned in an early chapter, you just have to start to observe. And ask and maybe just look for hints one level deeper than you used to be comfortable with.

Perhaps think of the question we raised in an earlier chapter, the role of clothing as money in a marriage. Or rather the power of clothing.

Some years ago, I came across an unusual story while I was writing one of many pieces I did about eBay. A woman in Texas was one of their Super Sellers, a level of seller that had surpassed others in volume of actual goods, sales totals, and quality of merchandise. On the surface, she looked to be a prototypical socialite. Her online store was chock full of Chanel suits and floral Oscar de la Renta tea dresses. The pictures that went with her listings were glossy and rarefied, as though shot by a *Vogue Italia* photographer. They displayed a manicured life of pristine white furniture, white carpeting, and chandeliers. She was skilled at leveraging the media coverage of her social appearances to get a premium on already-worn clothes, making more for them than she had paid. Her store was grossing thousands of dollars a month.

One day, while trying to follow up with her, I discovered her telephone number had changed. It transpired that her husband had been beating her and her two children for some years and that she had started the store in order to leave him. It was the only account not in both their names. The previous day, she had hit the amount of money she needed to take her children and start a new life. In a new city. With a new name. And since eBay leaves no search result footprints, and all transactions go through the PayPal layers, with one push of the delete button, her store disappeared.

Overnight, she was gone.

ACKNOWLEDGMENTS

THANK YOU to my parents: my father, who taught me the value of engineering and that many drops in the ocean turn into a tidal wave, and my mother, for her tireless efforts to improve the lives of others.

For all of his insights and brainstorming, it is beyond a privilege to have had the friendship and help of my brother on this book. A doctor, a consultant, a constant learner, who sees the world with unparalleled clarity and acuity, who challenges my thinking on global issues, and who I think is the person to fix some of the planet's greatest challenges. (No pressure.)

Without Linda Konner, my agent, and her wonderful directness, persistence, and guidance, and Suzanne Staszak-Silva, my wise editor, and her belief in me, *Disrobed* would not exist.

I would also like to thank Alan Chadwick, one of the best marketing minds of our time, as well as Gladys Felix, Will Hennessy, Michael Sokolow, Jamie Neidig, Karen Salmansohn, Jay Dixit, and the sharp thought leaders at McKinsey & Company. Thank you for helping me with research, legal perspectives, morale, sushi, laughs, and cocktails, and for answering the ten thousand e-mails that went into this book.

Gratitude goes out to my foreign rights agent, Betty Anne Crawford.

Thank you to Kathryn Knigge, Will True, Helen Subbio, Andrea Reider, Annette Van Deusen, and the energetic and tireless marketing and publicity teams at Rowman & Littlefield, especially Jacqline Barnes and Kelly Quarrinton.

NOTES

Introduction

1. Syl Tang, "Patriot Garments," *Financial Times*, December 29, 2007, www.ft.com/cms/s/0/59c44482-b5af-11dc-896e-0000779fd2ac.html.

2. While college is still considered valuable, the perception is that it has become too costly. "Is College Worth It?" Pew Research Center, May 15, 2011, http://www.pewsocialtrends.org/2011/05/15/is-college-worth-it/.

3. "Is College Worth It?" *Economist*, April 5, 2014, http://www.economist .com/news/united-states/21600131-too-many-degrees-are-waste-money -return-higher-education-would-be-much-better.

4. John Cassidy, "College Calculus," *New Yorker*, September 1, 2015, http:// www.newyorker.com/magazine/2015/09/07/college-calculus.

5. *GQ* has hilariously speculated that the sweatshirts may in fact be two-thousand-dollar Brunello Cucinellis. Jake Woolf, "Are Mark Zuckerberg's 'Everyman' Hoodies Actually Expensive-Ass Cashmere?" *GQ*, January 25, 2016, http://www.gq.com/story/mark-zuckerberg-facebook-hoodie-tee-gray-post.

6. Syl Tang, "Graffiti Girl Makes Her Mark on Fashion," *Financial Times*, August 27, 2005, https://www.ft.com/content/2bc441be-1696-11da -8081-00000e2511c8.

7. Medicom Toy Japan is just one of the officially licensed Banksy sculpture sources. See https://www.toytokyo.com/flower-bomber-by-banksy-medicom -toy-japan-official/.

8. Beatriz Valenzuela, "How the Security Team at Comic-Con Works to Keep Fans Safe," *Los Angeles Daily News*, July 16, 2016, http://www

.dailynews.com/arts-and-entertainment/20160716/how-the-security-team
-at-comic-con-works-to-keep-fans-safe.

9. "Cosplay by McCall's Sewing Patterns," 2017, accessed January 3, 2017, http://cosplay.mccall.com/. *Cosplay* is the merger of two words, "costume" and "play," and refers to the practice of dressing up as a character from a film, book, or video game, sometimes from Japanese genres manga and anime.

10. Actually first used by Ronald Reagan in 1983. Eric Garcia, "A History of 'Draining the Swamp,'" *Roll Call,* October 18, 2016, http://www.rollcall.com/news/politics/history-of-draining-the-swamp.

11. "2016 National Popular Vote Tracker," December 14, 2016, accessed January 2, 2017, http://cookpolitical.com/story/10174; Michael Kazin, "Trump and American Populism: Old Whine, New Bottles," *Foreign Affairs,* October 6, 2016, https://www.foreignaffairs.com/articles/united-states/2016-10-06/trump-and-american-populism.

12. Stan Greenberg, "Why Did Pollsters Like Me Fail to Predict Trump's Victory?" *Guardian,* November 19, 2016, https://www.theguardian.com/commentisfree/2016/nov/15/pollsters-fail-predict-trump-victory-fbi-clinton.

13. Ashley Kirk and Patrick Scott, "How Wrong Were the Polls in Predicting the US Election and Why Did They Fail to See Trump's Win?" *Telegraph,* November 17, 2016, http://www.telegraph.co.uk/news/2016/11/09/how-wrong-were-the-polls-in-predicting-the-us-election/.

14. John L. Beven II, Lixion A. Avila, Eric S. Blake, Daniel P. Brown, James L. Franklin, Richard D. Knabb, Richard J. Pasch, Jamie R. Rhome, and Stacy R. Stewart, "Annual Summary: Atlantic Hurricane Season of 2005," *Monthly Weather Review,* March 2008, http://www.aoml.noaa.gov/general/lib/lib1/nhclib/mwreviews/2005.pdf; Joan Brunkard, Gonza Namulanda, and Raoult Ratard, "Hurricane Katrina Deaths, Louisiana, 2005," *Disaster Medicine and Public Health Preparedness,* August 28, 2008, http://dhh.louisiana.gov/index.cfm/newsroom/category/10.

15. Syl Tang, "Mother Nature's Changing Style," *Financial Times,* September 29, 2006, http://hipguide.com/hipprint/pdf/FinancialTimes-9-29-06Rare.jpg.

16. Ibid.

17. Ibid.

18. Ibid.

19. David Derbyshire, "Scandal as Stores Pass Off Real Fur as Fake," *Daily Mail,* December 7, 2007, http://www.dailymail.co.uk/news/article-500185/Scandal-stores-pass-real-fur-fake.html.

20. Cherry Wilson, "REAL Fur Clothing Is Flying off a High Street Shelf Near You This Winter," *Sun,* December 21, 2015, accessed January 2, 2017, https://www.thesun.co.uk/archives/news/895386/real-fur-clothing-is-flying-off-a-high-street-shelf-near-you/; Ashitha Nagesh, "Debenhams Is Selling

Faux Fur That's Actually Real," *Metro.co.uk*, December 19, 2016, http://metro
.co.uk/2016/12/19/your-faux-fur-might-actually-be-real-6331864/.

21. The distance between New Orleans, Louisiana, and Dalston, London,
England.

Chapter 1

1. Syl Tang, "A Head Start on the Market," *Financial Times*, September 1,
2007, http://www.ft.com/cms/s/0/1fb00f94-5824-11dc-8c65-0000779fd2ac
.html.

2. Ibid.

3. Ibid.

4. Ibid.

5. *Investopedia*, s.v. "Case Study: The Collapse of Lehman Brothers," accessed
December 13, 2016, http://www.investopedia.com/articles/economics/09/
lehman-brothers-collapse.asp.

6. B. Ojalehto, S. R. Waxman, and D. L. Medin, "Teleological Reasoning
about Nature: Intentional Design or Relational Perspectives?" *Trends in Cogni-
tive Sciences*. 17, no. 4 (March 23, 2013), accessed December 13, 2016, https://
www.ncbi.nlm.nih.gov/pubmed/23518159.

7. "Number of Goldman Sachs Analysts Hired," May 2016, accessed
December 13, 2016, http://www.wallstreetoasis.com/forums/number-of
-goldman-sachs-analysts-hired. This average is available on a number of websites,
as provided by Goldman Sachs.

8. *Wikipedia*, s.v. "Financial Modeling," https://en.wikipedia.org/wiki/
Financial_modeling.

9. Jean Folger, *Investopedia*, s.v. "Options Pricing," http://www.investopedia
.com/university/options-pricing/.

10. Donald Saucier and Scott Fluke, "Research Project Offers Insight into
Superstitious Behavior," Kansas State University, https://www.k-state.edu/
media/newsreleases/sept10/superstition90210.html.

11. "Superstition: What the Pigeons Can Tell Us . . . ," *Psychologist World*,
http://www.psychologistworld.com/superstition_pigeons.php.

12. Syl Tang, "Amulets: A Helping Hand at the End of the World,"
Financial Times, November 13, 2009, https://www.ft.com/content/069460a8
-cf25-11de-8a4b-00144feabdc0.

13. Ibid.

14. Lysann Damisch, Barbara Stoberock, and Thomas Mussweiler, "Keep
Your Fingers Crossed! How Superstition Improves Performance," *Psychological
Science* 21, no. 7 (2010): 1014–20, doi: 10.1177/0956797610372631; Robert
J. Calin-Jageman and Tracy L. Caldwell, "Replication of the Superstition and

Performance Study by Damisch, Stoberock, and Mussweiler (2010)," *Social Psychology* 45, no. 3 (2014): 239–45, doi: 10.1027/1864-9335/a000190.

15. Harold G. Koenig, *Medicine, Religion, and Health: Where Science and Spirituality Meet* (Cincinnati, OH: Templeton Foundation Press, 2014).

16. "Francis Galton," *Biography.com*, accessed December 13, 2016, http://www.biography.com/people/francis-galton-9305647.

17. Biologist Richard Dawkins later concluded that this might have been due to "performance anxiety": "Am I so sick that people need to pray for me?"

18. Interview with Kenneth J. Lane by Syl Tang, August 12, 2014.

19. Since the Pope has to store his actual jeweled crucifix every evening for safekeeping, the designer made him one he could even wear "in the toilet."

20. Yan Zhang, Jane L. Risen, and Christine Hosey, "Reversing One's Fortune by Pushing Away Bad Luck," *Journal of Experimental Psychology: General* 143, no. 3 (June 2014): 1171–84.

21. Syl Tang, "Weapons of Distraction," *Financial Times*, October 28, 2006, http://www.ft.com/cms/s/0/fa77320c-6620-11db-a4fc-0000779e2340.html.

22. Antonio Damasio, "When Emotions Make Better Decisions," https://www.youtube.com/watch?v=1wup_K2WN0I.

23. Naomi Leach, "What Could Possibly Go Wrong? Passenger Carrying Handbag with a GUN Design on It Is Stopped by German Airport Officials," http://www.dailymail.co.uk/travel/travel_news/article-3181269/What-possibly-wrong-Passenger-carrying-handbag-GUN-design-stopped-German-airport-officials.html#ixzz4YlhbIRTd.

24. Ted Cox, "Chicago Moves to Ban Gun-Shaped Cellphone Cases," https://www.dnainfo.com/chicago/20150713/downtown/chicago-moves-ban-gun-shaped-cellphone-cases.

25. Lisa Eppich, "You Can Get Arrested for Wearing an Awesome Ring to the Airport," *Refinery29*, http://www.refinery29.com/shepard-fairey-ring-does-not-obey-the-law-will-get-you-arrested-at-the-airport.

26. Robert Todd Carroll, *The Skeptic's Dictionary: A Collection of Strange Beliefs, Amusing Deceptions, and Dangerous Delusions* (Hoboken, NJ: John Wiley and Sons, 2003).

27. This number will increase by around 6,200; "Nielsen Announces Significant Expansion to Sample Sizes in Local Television Markets," Nielsen Press Room, http://www.nielsen.com/us/en/press-room/2014/nielsen-announces-significant-expansion-to-sample-sizes-in-local-tv-markets.html.

28. "MTA Subway Facts and Figures," MTA, accessed December 13, 2016, http://web.mta.info/nyct/facts/ffsubway.htm.

29. Anna Vital, "Why We Live: Counting the People Your Life Impacts," *Funders and Founders*, http://fundersandfounders.com/counting-the-people-you-impact/.

30. Max Weber, "The Nature of Social Action," in W. G. Runciman, *Weber: Selections in Translation* (Cambridge: Cambridge University Press, 1991), 7–32.

31. Claude S. Fischer, *To Dwell among Friends: Personal Networks in Town and City* (Chicago: University of Chicago Press, 1991).

32. W. Thalheimer, "How Much Do People Forget?" http://willthalheimer .typepad.com/files/how-much-do-people-forget-v12-14-2010-2.pdf.

33. Syl Tang, "Totally Grandpa," *Financial Times*, October 18, 2008, https:// www.ft.com/content/f5d0bb2c-9cad-11dd-a42e-000077b07658.

34. Masanori Sakaguchi and Yasunori Hayashi, "Catching the Engram: Strategies to Examine the Memory Trace," *Molecular Brain*, http://molecularbrain .biomedcentral.com/articles/10.1186/1756-6606-5-32.

35. Wikipedia, s.v. "Vivos (Underground Shelter)," accessed November 1, 2016, https://en.wikipedia.org/wiki/Vivos_(underground_shelter); Everett Rosenfeld, "Apocalypse Later: Largest Bunker Scrapped," *CNBC*, July 3, 2014, http://www.cnbc.com/2014/07/03/apocalypse-later-largest-bunker-scrapped .html.

36. Sophie Jane Evans, "Vivos Builds $1 Billion Luxury Underground Bunker in German Village," *Daily Mail*, June 14, 2015, http://www.dailymail .co.uk/news/article-3123296/The-ultimate-doomsday-escape-California -entrepreneur-builds-1billion-luxury-underground-bunker-tiny-German -village-millionaires-event-apocalypse-survivors-live-year-without-leaving .html.

Chapter 2

1. Roger Drummer Fisher, William Ury, and Bruce Patton, *Getting to Yes: Negotiating Agreement without Giving In*, second ed. (New York: Penguin Group, 2006).

2. The name itself is a con we all go along with.

3. Top result went to a Paco Rabanne dress that fetched over $24,000. See "Resurrection: Avant-Garde Fashion," http://www.christies.com/lotfinder/ searchresults.aspx?intSaleID=22039#action=refine&intSaleID=22039&sid=28 301abf-aac5-4291-8e33-0918fcc8b606.

4. Ibid.

5. There has been an incredible amount written on McLaren's claims, but Haidee Findlay-Levin gives extensive detail on design issues with visual support in her August 2008 post, "Punk Private Eye," *Hintmag.com*, accessed December 16, 2016, http://www.hintmag.com/blog/.

6. Syl Tang, "Anarchy at the Auction," *Financial Times*, October 25, 2008, www.ft.com/cms/s/0/3823fe6e-a22e-11dd-a32f-000077b07658.html.

7. Original interview by me, October 1, 2008, at length with Malcolm McLaren directly (henceforth cited as October 1, 2008, interview). I conducted one of the longest interviews McLaren gave on this topic, the original transcript of which is with the *Financial Times*. This battle that he waged has been extensively covered, and it continues with the estate of his longtime

companion, Young Kim. It was covered again in 2013 when the Metropolitan Museum mounted a punk-themed exhibit: Edward Helmore, "Malcolm McLaren's Widow Fears Metropolitan Museum of Art Will Get Punk Fashion Show All Wrong," *Guardian*, February 16, 2013, https://www.theguardian .com/fashion/2013/feb/16/punk-fashion-gets-it-wrong.

8. Craig Bromberg, *The Wicked Ways of Malcolm McLaren: Sex Pistols, Boy George, Adam Ant, Butterfly, Bow Wow Wow, Buffalo Gals, Too Fast to Live, Too Young to Die* (New York: HarperCollins Publishers, 1989).

9. Ian Macleay, *Malcolm McLaren: The Sex Pistols, the Anarchy, the Art, the Genius—The Whole Amazing Legacy* (London: John Blake Publishing, 2010).

10. Ibid.

11. McLaren, October 1, 2008, interview.

12. After McLaren's death in 2010, Young Kim and historian Paul Gorman took up the fight and continued to document it, as seen here in Gorman's blog post. As a result, they have won removal of some pieces and changes in attribution. See Paul Gorman, "Trouble at the Met: Status of Half of the Punk Collection Downgraded but Dubious Designs Continue to Toxify Costume Institute Collection," Paul Gorman, December 10, 2016, accessed December 16, 2016, http://www.paulgormanis.com/?p=11464.

13. Paul Gorman, Paul Smith, and Malcolm McLaren, *The Look: Adventures in Rock and Pop Fashion* (London: Adelita, 2006).

14. Tang, "Anarchy."

15. "Punk/Rock," http://www.christies.com/SaleLanding/index.aspx?intSaleID =21700&lid=1.

16. Tang, "Anarchy."

17. The sale fetched £270,925. For sale results, see "Resurrection: Avant-Garde Fashion," http://www.christies.com/lotfinder/searchresults.aspx?intSale ID=22039#action=refine&intSaleID=22039&sid=28301abf-aac5-4291 -8e33-0918fcc8b606, which comprised thirty-two Westwood items, many fetching over £1000.

18. Young Kim, personal communication, October 25, 2008.

19. Journalist and punk chronicler Paul Gorman has in his archives the letters that McLaren famously wrote to the press during the Sex Pistols years.

20. "Rush and Molloy: 'Artist Punked by Fake Duds,'" *Daily News*, July 28, 2008, accessed December 16, 2016, http://www.nydailynews.com/entertain ment/gossip/artist-punked-fake-duds-article-1.346761.

21. Kris Hollington, "Are You Feeling Lucky Punk?" *Daily Mail*, August 28, 2008, http://www.dailymail.co.uk/home/moslive/article-1046965/Are-feeling -lucky-punk.html.

22. Punkpistol.com is a website owned by clothing dealer Simon Easton.

23. Coffee-table book publisher Rizzoli had at that juncture a book in process, called *Punk Couture: Clothes for Heroes*, written by dealer Simon Easton.

24. The Costume Institute's exhibits are still shown in the basement.

25. "Rush and Molloy: 'Artist Punked.'"

26. Running since 1979, this show has more than seven international versions with countless spin-offs, such as *Bargain Hunt*.

27. "Frasier Online Episode Guide: Episode 7.07—A Tsar Is Born," accessed December 16, 2016, http://www.frasieronline.co.uk/episodeguide/season7/ep7.htm.

28. Death and Co. keeps threatening to do just that: get shut down or die out. So forgive me if it's gone (or gone and reopened and gone and reopened) by the time you read this.

29. Just a few short online reviews from bar-goers:

- Guidespot, Los Angeles: "It doesn't get much more authentic than Cedd Moses' speakeasy" (May 26, 2009)
- My Little Secret, New York: "The newish Little Italy speakeasy . . . an authentic speakeasy from New York's Prohibition hey-day"
- Scranton Reads presents The Speakeasy: "Scranton Reads will recreate the Prohibition-era setting of the book with an authentic speakeasy."
- Speakeasy San Francisco: "I love how they recreate an authentic speakeasy experience. The fact that this is the site of a real Prohibition Era speakeasy certainly adds. . . ."
- Plight of the Pumpernickel: The Gibson: A Great Bar and A Not So, Washington, DC: "Drinks were exceptional; their list is mind-boggling, and speakeasy authentic to boot. The cocktails offered are all original to the 1920s" (November 19, 2009)

30. This fiction is further edified in other fiction. In "Last Call," an episode of the popular TV series *Castle*, the title character buys up a bar called The Old Haunt while telling inaccurate stories of the "glamorous" speakeasy era.

31. The original SHRM study in May 2010 is no longer on their site, however it has been widely cited, including here: "More Than Half of Job Applicants Lie on Their Resumes," 2010, http://www.workplaceethicsadvice.com/2012/08/more-than-half-of-job-applicants-lie-on-their-resumes-advice-for-employers-to-deal-with-manipulated-resume-information-a.html. In 2015, SHRM conducted another study and found similar results; see Kathy Gurchiek, "Liar, Liar, Resume on Fire," February 9, 2015, accessed December 16, 2016, https://www.shrm.org/resourcesandtools/hr-topics/talent-acquisition/pages/lying-exaggerating-padding-resume.aspx.

32. Graham Bowley and Colin Moynihan, "Knoedler Gallery Heads to Trial in Sale of a Fake Rothko," *New York Times*, January 26, 2016, http://www

.nytimes.com/2016/01/25/arts/design/knoedler-gallery-heads-to-trial-in-sale-of-a-fake-rothko.html?_r=0.

33. Syl Tang, "A Particularly Low Form of Flattery," *Financial Times,* April 30, 2005, https://www.ft.com/content/bf57adce-b914-11d9-bfeb-00000e2511c8.

34. "Copying: Fair or Unfair?" *Intangible Business,* 2003, accessed December 16, 2016, http://www.intangiblebusiness.com/reports/copying--fair-or-unfair-/828.

35. *Wikipedia,* s.v. "Hwang Woo-suk," accessed December 16, 2016, https://en.wikipedia.org/wiki/Hwang_Woo-suk.

36. Hwang was dismissed on March 20, 2006.

37. "A Cloning Scandal Rocks a Pillar of Science Publishing," *New York Times,* December 18, 2005, http://www.nytimes.com/learning/teachers/featured_articles/20051220tuesday.html.

38. Syl Tang, "Ebay Helps Conjure Up Spirit of Orleans," *Financial Times,* January 2006, http://hipguide.com/hipprint/pdf/FinancialTimes-1-28-06ShoppingAfterKatrina.jpg.

39. Katie Benner and Christopher Tkaczyk, "Eight Who Saw It Coming," *Fortune,* August 2008, http://archive.fortune.com/galleries/2008/fortune/0808/gallery.whosawitcoming.fortune; "Dr. Doom," *New York Times,* August 15, 2008, http://www.nytimes.com/2008/08/17/magazine/17pessimist-t.html.

40. Edward M. Gramlich, *Subprime Mortgages: America's Latest Boom and Bust* (Washington, DC: Urban Institute Press, 2008).

41. Gary A. Shilling, "The Pin That Bursts the Housing Bubble," *Forbes,* July 21, 2005, http://www.forbes.com/2005/07/21/lennar-hovnanian-kb-cz_ags_0721soapbox_inl.html.

42. A mortgage-backed security (MBS) is an asset-backed security or debt obligation that represents a claim on the cash flows from mortgage loans through a process known as *securitization.*

43. MoneyTree Report from PricewaterhouseCoopers LLP (PwC) and the National Venture Capital Association (NVCA), based on data provided by Thomson Reuters.

44. Ellie Ismailidou, "Delivering Alpha Live Blog Recap: Billionaire Investors Paint Gloomy Picture for Economy, Markets," September 13, 2016, accessed December 16, 2016, http://blogs.marketwatch.com/thetell/2016/09/13/live-blog-icahn-chanos-singer-at-delivering-alpha/.

45. Serena Saitto, "Uber Raises $1.6 Billion in Convertible Debt to Expand," *Bloomberg,* January 21, 2015, https://www.bloomberg.com/news/articles/2015-01-21/uber-said-to-raise-1-6-billion-in-convertible-debt-to-expand.

46. Sarah Lacy, "Peter Thiel on Why Airbnb Should Be Valued Way Higher Than Uber...And Why It's Not," October 7, 2014, accessed December 16, 2016, https://pando.com/2014/10/07/peter-thiel-on-why-airbnb-should-be-valued-way-higher-than-uber-and-why-its-not/; Drew Sandholm, "VCs Bill Gurley,

Peter Thiel Clash over Uber," *CNBC*, July 12, 2016, http://www.cnbc.com/2014/11/03/vcs-bill-gurley-peter-thiel-clash-over-uber.html.

47. "Uber Valued at about $51 Billion After Latest Funding Round: WSJ," *Reuters*, July 31, 2015, accessed December 16, 2016, http://www.reuters.com/article/us-uber-valuation-idUSKCN0Q52DM20150731.

48. Aaron Pressman, "Snapchat, Uber, and Palantir: Why 2017's IPO Market Could Be Huge." *Fortune,* November 16, 2016, accessed December 16, 2016, http://fortune.com/2016/11/16/snapchat-uber-palantir-ipo/.

Chapter 3

1. Phoebe Eaton, "Saving Graces," *New York Magazine*, May 1, 1989, https://books.google.com/books?id=CugCAAAAMBAJ&pg=PA122&lpg=PA122&dq=jackie+onassis+michael%27s+resale&source=bl&ots=m3hhfgL234&sig=uw2nPq0KLJqP8AsVMo7poLKqsP0&hl=en&sa=X&ved=0ahUKEwiQnfy0y_HQAhVHOMAKHfrnAmEQ6AEIRjAG#v=onepage&q=jackie%20onassis%20michael%27s%20resale&f=false. Also, Tiffany Yannetta, "Ten Consignment Shops Every Sample Sale Junkie Should Know," *Racked.com*, July 31, 2012, accessed December 13, 2016, http://ny.racked.com/2012/7/31/7717329/10-nyc-consignment-shops. And "Second Hand and Thrift Stores in NYC," *Fodor's Travel*, February 20, 2000, accessed December 13, 2016, http://www.fodors.com/community/united-states/second-hand-thrift-stores-in-nyc.cfm.

2. Syl Tang, "Cashing in on Cast-Offs," *Financial Times*, March 21, 2009, https://www.ft.com/content/3c3fbd4c-15b7-11de-b9a9-0000779fd2ac.

3. Syl Tang, "Pedal Power," *Financial Times,* June 28, 2008, www.ft.com/cms/s/0/003c4fa4-44ac-11dd-b151-0000779fd2ac.html.

4. "Use of Time for Outdoor Recreation in the United States, 1965–2007," May 14, 2009, http://www.rff.org/research/publications/use-time-outdoor-recreation-united-states-1965-2007.

5. This should not be confused with visitation to national parks or actual individual participation rates, which has largely stayed the same. See Margaret Walls, "Parks and Recreation in the United States," June 2009, http://www.rff.org/files/sharepoint/WorkImages/Download/RFF-BCK-ORRG_Local%20Parks.pdf.

6. Disclaimer: such as the author's own original guide.

7. Fitbit has since had an IPO valued at $358 million and trades on the NYSE.

8. Physicist Richard S. Lindzen criticized Gore for presenting a biased view. NASA climate model-maker Gavin Schmidt expressed concern about Gore's lack of distinction between correlation and causation. University of Miami's meteorology professor Brian Soden indicated some concern about the use of Hurricane Katrina.

9. The program is now called Santander Cycles. Barclays Bank sponsored the program from 2010 till 2015 when Santander took over as title sponsor.

10. The city experienced its first fatality that year.

11. Syl Tang, "Sign of the Times," *Financial Times*. This figure appears in the original article, which ran on March 8, 2008, and was provided by Danny Bitran, spokesperson for Nahui Ollin. It is also available in the original verbatim transcript. An abbreviated version of the article has been archived on ft.com at http://www.ft.com/cms/s/0/37ccfeb6-ecb2-11dc-86be -0000779fd2ac.html.

12. "Pay Equity & Discrimination," Institute for Women's Policy Research, 2010, accessed December 13, 2016, http://www.iwpr.org/initiatives/ pay-equity-and-discrimination.

13. "The Simple Truth about the Gender Pay Gap (Spring 2017)," AAUW, http://www.aauw.org/research/the-simple-truth-about-the-gender-pay-gap.

14. Ibid.

15. US Bureau of Labor Statistics, "Household Data Annual Averages," Table 39, Median weekly earnings of full-time wage and salary workers by detailed occupation and sex, 2016, http://www.bls.gov/cps/cpsaat39.pdf.

16. "The Simple Truth."

17. "Chore Wars: Men, Women and Housework," 2005 time-diary data from the federally funded Panel Study of Income Dynamics, University of Michigan Institute for Social Research (ISR), National Science Foundation, http:// www.nsf.gov/discoveries/disc_images.jsp?cntn_id=111458, featuring University of Michigan economist Frank Stafford; Diane Swanbrow, "Exactly How Much Housework Does a Husband Create?" *Michigan News*, April 3, 2008, http://ns.umich.edu/new/releases/6452.

18. A partial transcript appears in Tang, "Cashing in on Cast-Offs."

19. This is a conclusion from my interview with Lili Vasileff, which appears in Tang, "Cashing in on Cast-Offs"; however, this has also been widely documented by historians in books about Jacqueline Kennedy Onassis, including former Secret Service agent Clint Hill's *Mrs. Kennedy and Me: An Intimate Memoir*; online by Elios Patronikolas in his blog about Aristotle Onassis, October 1, 2007, http://aristotle-onassis.blogspot.com/2007/10/aristotle-onassis -why-he-wanted.html; and in a television special entitled *A&E Biography: Jacqueline Kennedy Onassis*, a summary of which can be found at http://www .biography.com/people/jacqueline-kennedy-onassis-9428644.

20. Wednesday Martin, *Primates of Park Avenue: A Memoir* (New York: Simon and Schuster, 2015).

21. Studies show that the majority of people self-identify as middle-class, whether they make $10K or $150K. See, for example, the November 9–12, 2012, *USA Today*/Gallup poll cited in Andrew Dugan, "Americans Most Likely to Say They Belong to the Middle Class," November 30, 2012, http://www. gallup.com/poll/159029/americans-likely-say-belong-middle-class.aspx.

22. For our purposes here, "affluent" is defined as households with discretionary incomes of $250K or more to spend on pastimes, not fixed costs, as per the American Express Publishing Survey of Affluence and Wealth in America.

23. "Off the Deep End: The Wall Street Bonus Pool and Low-Wage Workers," Institute for Policy Studies, March 8, 2016, http://www.ips-dc.org/wp-content/uploads/2016/03/Wall-Street-bonuses-v-minimum-wage-2016-FINAL.pdf.

Chapter 4

1. Syl Tang, "Second-Hand, Not Second-Rate," *Financial Times,* July 19, 2008.

2. Facebook was founded February 4, 2004, according to their NASDAQ filing, accessed August 8, 2016.

3. Accessed June 8, 2016, https://www.freecycle.org/. At the time of my article, Freecycle had 4,906,000 members.

4. Based on data available through the New York State Department of Environmental Conservation (NYSDEC), New York State's environmental protection and regulatory agency.

5. Data provided by Christopher Ward, Department of Environmental Protection, http://www1.nyc.gov/.

6. Statistic provided by Warren Liebold at Conservation for New York.

7. United Nations, Framework Convention on Climate Change, http://unfccc.int/meetings/paris_nov_2015/meeting/8926.php. I also wrote about this in the *Financial Times* with regard to the Philippines in 2015.

8. World Bank, http://www.worldbank.org/en/topic/environment/brief/pollution.

9. Brian Merchant, "How Many Gallons of Water Does It Take . . .," *TreeHugger*, http://www.treehugger.com/clean-technology/how-many-gallons-of-water-does-it-take-to-make.html; Water Use It Wisely, "It Takes 1,800 Gallons of Water to Make One Pair of Jeans," http://wateruseitwisely.com/it-takes-1800-gallons-of-water-to-make-one-pair-of-jeans/.

10. "Thirteen Fun Facts About Water," *Audubon Magazine*, National Audubon Society, November 2012, https://www.audubon.org/magazine/november-december-2012/thirteen-fun-facts-about-water.

11. This oft-cited medical recommendation is an approximate, as reiterated by the Mayo Clinic, "Water: How Much Should You Drink Every Day?" http://www.mayoclinic.org/healthy-lifestyle/nutrition-and-healthy-eating/in-depth/water/art-20044256.

12. HM alone donates more than half a million items of unsold clothing to charity each year, not inclusive of clothing the company states does not meet safety standards.

13. Justin Brandt, Michelle Sneed, Laurel Lynn Rogers, Loren F. Metzger, Diane Rewis, and Sally House, "Water Use in California," USGS California Water Science Center, 2014, doi:10.5066/F7KD1VXV.

14. "Residential End Uses of Water," American Water Works Association Research Foundation, 1999, https://www3.epa.gov/watersense/docs/ws_indoor508.pdf, http://www.waterrf.org/publicreportlibrary/rfr90781_1999_241a.pdf.

15. "California Drought," USGS California Water Science Center, November 3, 2016, https://ca.water.usgs.gov/data/drought/.

16. Samantha Storey, "How to Save Water: The California Way," *New York Times*, April 2, 2015, www.nytimes.com/interactive/2015/04/03/us/california-drought-how-to-save-water.html?_r=1.

17. Dennis Diaz, "California Drought Has Been Good for Laundry Business," *Eastern Funding Blog*, August 10, 2015, http://blog.easternfunding.com/california-drought-has-been-good-for-laundry-business.

18. Carlo Calma, "How California Drought Impacts State's Coin Laundry Industry," *American Coinop*, August 3, 2015, https://americancoinop.com/articles/how-california-drought-impacts-states-coin-laundry-industry-part-1.

19. Valerie Flynn, "EU Countries Agree Textile Chemical Ban," *Guardian*, July 21, 2015, https://www.theguardian.com/environment/2015/jul/21/eu-countries-agree-textile-chemical-ban; "Polluting Paradise," Greenpeace, accessed August 18, 2016, http://www.greenpeace.org/international/en/campaigns/detox/water/polluting-paradise/.

20. Leo Hickman, "Is it OK . . . to Dry-Clean Your Clothes?" *Guardian*, November 14, 2005, http://www.theguardian.com/money/2005/nov/15/ethicalmoney.

21. Brian Dakss, "Cancer Danger from Dry Cleaning?" *CBS*, February 23, 2007, http://www.cbsnews.com/news/cancer-danger-from-dry-cleaning/.

22. According to a January 2016 McKinsey slide presentation, eBay has even started to expand into an off-line presence by testing physical stores in midsize cities such as Bilbao, Spain; Jorge Omeñaca, "Global Trends of Non-Food in the Grocery Channel," *McKinsey & Company*, January 2016.

23. Felix Richter, "The U.S. Apparel Industry," Statista, September 2, 2014, https://www.statista.com/chart/2657/the-us-apparel-industry.

24. Ibid.

25. A timeline for the Target collections can be seen here: http://www.racked.com/2012/6/25/7720279/targets-collab-history-a-timeline.

26. Yoram Gutgeld, Ingeborg Hegstad, Stefanie Sauer, and Tobias Wachinger, "Addressing the Hypermarket Dilemma," *McKinsey & Company*, December 2009.

27. It would be a mistake not to consider that the economy post-2008 had a factor in people seeking out value, as well as high gas prices. However, the movement toward discounters existed during the better economic years of '05 and '06, as well as now, with lowered gas prices.

28. Omeñaca, "Global Trends."

29. This is down from its peak of around 40 percent in 2008–2009; the drop is largely due to the fact that gold prices aren't that high now. Gabriel Motta, Greg Callaway, and Ignace Proot, "Gold Supply Outlook 2025, Basic Materials Practice I Commodity Perspective," *McKinsey & Company*, July/August 2016.

30. Tim Nudd, "The Brand Declares War on Consumerism Gone Berserk, and Admits Its Own Environmental Failings," *Adweek*, November 28, 2011, http://www.adweek.com/news/advertising-branding/ad-day-patagonia-136745.

31. "Bring Back the Holidays: Pumpkin Pie," television commercial, T. J. Maxx, https://www.youtube.com/watch?v=gMRRyqXoJOw.

32. The REI Opt Outside campaign: http://optoutside.rei.com/.

33. Rose Marcario, "The Most Eco-Friendly Clothes Are the Ones Already in Your Closet," *Quartz*, November 25, 2015, http://qz.com/553614/the-most-eco-friendly-clothes-are-the-ones-already-in-your-closet/.

34. There are countless articles about Marie Kondo, but one in particular does a good job of summarizing her impact, the perception of the "movement" by other professional organizers, as well as the cultish following that surrounds her method. See Taffy Brodesser-Anker, "Marie Kondo and the Ruthless War on Stuff," *New York Times Magazine*, July 6, 2016, http://www.nytimes.com/2016/07/10/magazine/marie-kondo-and-the-ruthless-war-on-stuff.html?_r=0.

35. "Europe's Circular-Economy Opportunity," McKinsey Center for Business and Environment, September 2015.

36. The idea supposedly started either in 1976, 1982, or 1989. Walter Stahel and Genevieve Reday presented in 1976 a Hannah Reekman research report to the European Commission, "The Potential for Substituting Manpower for Energy," which according to "Cradle to Cradle: The Product-Life Institute" (Product-life.org, November 14, 2012) was then published as a 1982 book titled *Jobs for Tomorrow: The Potential for Substituting Manpower for Energy*. The notion of recycling was then further discussed by British economists David W. Pearce and R. Kerry Turner in their 1989 book *Economics of Natural Resources and the Environment*. But it is not really until 2007, when an article by F. Zhijun and Y. Nailing, "Putting a Circular Economy into Practice in China" (*Sustainability Science* 2:95–101), suggests it as national policy in China's eleventh Five-Year Plan, that the term starts to exist.

37. "Europe's Circular-Economy Opportunity," McKinsey Center for Business and Environment, September 2015.

38. World Bank figures for GDP growth by nation: http://data.worldbank.org/indicator/NY.GDP.MKTP.KD.ZG.

39. "China's Consumers," *Economist*, April 30, 2016, http://www.economist.com/news/business-and-finance/21697597-free-spending-consumers-provide-comfort-troubled-economy-consumption-china-resilient; Jeffrey Towson and Jonathan Woetzel, "Why China's Consumers Will Continue to Surprise the World," *McKinsey & Company*, May 2015, http://www.mckinsey.com/

business-functions/strategy-and-corporate-finance/our-insights/why-chinas
-consumers-will-continue-to-surprise-the-world; Eswar Prasad, transcript of
testimony to the US-China Economic and Security Review Commission, "The
Path to Sustainable Growth in China," April 22, 2015, https://www.brookings
.edu/testimonies/the-path-to-sustainable-growth-in-china/.

40. United Nations, Framework Convention on Climate Change, http://
unfccc.int/meetings/paris_nov_2015/meeting/8926.php; Chris Mooney and
Steven Mufson, "In a Major Moment for Climate Policy, China, Brazil, and the
U.S. All Announce New Commitments," *Economist,* June 30, 2015; "China
Announces New Long-Term Commitment to Curb Climate Change," NRDC,
June 30, 2015, https://www.nrdc.org/media/2015/150630.

41. Matt Williams, "What Percent of Earth Is Water?" Phys.org, accessed
December 13, 2016, http://phys.org/news/2014-12-percent-earth.html.

42. Data provided by Christopher Ward, Department of Environmental
Protection, http://www.nyc.gov.

Chapter 5

1. Katy McLaughlin, "A New King of the Food World," *Wall Street Journal,*
June 18, 2010, http://www.wsj.com/articles/SB10001424052748704575304575296501799403866.

2. Kristin Tice Studeman, "Inside the New Noma," *Vogue,* February 18,
2016, http://www.vogue.com/13402800/noma-rene-redzepi-australia-pop-up
-restaurant-interview/.

3. I counted no fewer than thirteen articles in the *Guardian* singing the
praises of Noma. Just a few are: Jay Rayner, "Why It's Cooler in the North,"
May 23, 2009, http://www.theguardian.com/lifeandstyle/2009/may/24/noma
-restaurant-copenhagen-jay-rayner; Tim Lewis, "Claus Meyer: The Other Man
from Noma," March 20, 2016, http://www.theguardian.com/lifeandstyle/2016/
mar/20/claus-meyer-the-other-man-from-noma-copenhagen-nordic-kitchen
-recipes; Elle Hunt, "Noma Sydney: Diners Go to Extreme Lengths to Secure
Spot at Sellout Pop-Up Restaurant," January 26, 2016, http://www.theguardian
.com/lifeandstyle/2016/jan/27/noma-sydney-diners-go-to-extreme-lengths-to
-secure-spot-at-sellout-pop-up-restaurant.

4. Joe Ray, "Culinary Copenhagen," *Boston Globe,* July 12, 2006, http://
archive.boston.com/travel/articles/2006/07/12/culinary_copenhagen/?page
=full.

5. Teresa Levonian Cole, "Hungry Traveler," *Telegraph,* August 21, 2006,
http://www.telegraph.co.uk/travel/destinations/europe/denmark/736101/
Hungry-traveller.html.

6. Jonathan Hayes, "Manifesto for a New Nordic Cuisine," *Food and Wine,*
http://www.foodandwine.com/articles/manifesto-for-a-new-nordic-cuisine.

7. "New Nordic Food Ambassador Wins Prize," Nordic Council of Ministers, December 11, 2008, http://www.norden.org/en/news-and-events/news/new-nordic-food-ambassador-wins-prize/.

8. "Christopher McCandless Bio," http://www.christophermccandless.info/bio.html.

9. Jon Krakauer, *Into the Wild* (New York: Villard, 1996).

10. Bri Kelly at Thompson PR, the agency of record for the State of Alaska told me when I traveled to Alaska in 2014 that, to their chagrin and dismay, the state fields countless requests, expressions of curiosity, and trips around McCandless's journey.

11. Audubon Society, *Field Guide to North American Mushrooms* (New York: Alfred A. Knopf, 1981).

12. C. M. Stein, P. E. Wu, J. A. Scott, and A. S. Weinerman, "Fulminant Hepatic Failure Following Ingestion of Wild Mushrooms." *Canadian Medical Association Journal*, August 11, 2015, http://atlasofscience.org/foraging-gone-wrong-a-case-of-poisoning-from-wild-mushrooms/.

13. Cat Adams, "The Most Dangerous Mushroom," *Slate*, February 10, 2014, http://www.slate.com/articles/health_and_science/medical_examiner/2014/02/most_dangerous_mushroom_death_cap_is_spreading_but_poisoning_can_be_treated.html.

14. Judith A. Stock, "Hunt, Gather, Sauté," *Full-Service Restaurant*, May 2013, https://www.fsrmagazine.com/sustainability/hunt-gather-saut?page=2.

15. Sierra Tishgart, "Into the Wild: 8 New York Restaurants Where You Can Find Truly Foraged Foods," *New York Magazine*, February 20, 2013, http://www.grubstreet.com/2013/02/new-york-restaurants-foraged-food.html.

16. See http://www.viamichelin.com/web/Restaurants/Restaurants-United_States, retrieved July 7, 2016.

17. See "What Is the Farm-to-Table Movement?" Culinaryschools.com, last updated September 9, 2013, http://www.culinaryschools.com/farm-to-table-movement; Bruce Schoenfeld, "The Farm-to-Table Founding Fathers," *Entrepreneur*, September 21, 2011, https://www.entrepreneur.com/article/220392; "Farm to Table," *Restaurant-ing through History*, January 19, 2016, https://restaurant-ingthroughhistory.com/2016/01/19/farm-to-table/.

18. "The Birth of Locavore," *OUPblog*, November 20, 2007, http://blog.oup.com/2007/11/prentice/.

19. This is from articles where she is quoted. More accurately *loco* or *locus* is "place," "spot," or "position" in Latin; the Latin for "local" is *locorus*.

20. CSA is community-supported agriculture, basically owning shares in a local farm from which your profit-sharing is food.

21. Food and Agriculture Organization of the United Nations, FAO Rural Infrastructure and Agro-industries Division, "Labour," retrieved August 23, 2016, http://www.fao.org/docrep/015/i2490e/i2490e01b.pdf.

22. The Cotton Board, "About," http://www.cottonboard.org/about/; Cotton Board press release, "The Cotton Board Recommends $76 Million Cotton Incorporated Budget to Secretary of Agriculture," August 14, 2015, http://www.cottonboard.org/news/press-releases/-the-cotton-board-recommends-76-million-cotton-incorporated-budget-to-secretary-of-agriculture/.

23. S. C. Fang, A. J. Mehta, J. Q. Hang, E. A. Eisen, H. L. Dai, H. X. Zhang, L Su, D. C. Christiani, "Cotton Dust, Endotoxin and Cancer Mortality among the Shanghai Textile Workers Cohort: A 30-Year Analysis," National Institutes of Health, http://www.ncbi.nlm.nih.gov/pmc/articles/PMC3805789/#; G. Astrakianakis, N. S. Seixas, R. Ray, J. E. Camp, D. L. Gao, Z. Feng, W. Li, K. J. Wernli, E. D. Fitzgibbons, D. B. Thomas, and H. Checkoway, "Lung Cancer Risk among Female Textile Workers Exposed to Endotoxin," *Journal of the National Cancer Institute,* March 7, 2007; K. J. Wernli, R. M. Ray, D. L. Gao, E. D. Fitzgibbons, J. E. Camp, G. Astrakianakis, N. Seixas, E. Y. Wong, W. Li, A. J. De Roos, et al., "Occupational Exposures and Ovarian Cancer in Textile Workers," *Epidemiology,* March 19, 2008; K. J. Wernli, E. D. Fitzgibbons, R. M. Ray, D. L. Gao, W. Li, N. S. Seixas, J. E. Camp, G. Astrakianakis G, Z. Feng, D. B. Thomas, et al., "Occupational Risk Factors for Esophageal and Stomach Cancers among Female Textile Workers in Shanghai, China," *American Journal of Epidemiology* 163, no. 8 (April 15, 2006):717–25; C. K. Chang, G. Astrakianakis, D. B. Thomas, N. S. Seixas, R. M. Ray, D. L. Gao, K. J. Wernli, E. D. Fitzgibbons, T. L. Vaughan, and H. Checkoway, "Occupational Exposures and Risks of Liver Cancer among Shanghai Female Textile Workers—a Case-Cohort Study," *International Journal of Epidemiology* 35, no. 2 (April 2006): 361–69; V. Lenters, I. Basinas, L. Beane-Freeman, P. Boffetta, H. Checkoway, D. Coggon, L. Portengen, M. Sim, I. M. Wouters, D. Heederik, et al. "Endotoxin Exposure and Lung Cancer Risk: A Systematic Review and Meta-Analysis of the Published Literature on Agriculture and Cotton Textile Workers," *Cancer Causes Control* 21, no. 4 (April 2010): 523–55; P. S. Lai and D. C. Christiani, "Long-Term Respiratory Health Effects in Textile Workers," *Current Opinion in Pulmonary Medicine* 19, no. 2 (March 2013): 152–57.

24. "The Deadly Chemicals in Cotton," Environmental Justice Foundation, 2007, http://ejfoundation.org/report/deadly-chemicals-cotton.

25. The United States Department of Agriculture's Foreign Agriculture Service monthly cotton report includes data on US and global trade, production, consumption, and stocks, as well as analysis of developments affecting world trade in cotton. It breaks down thoroughly worldwide demand and fluctuations country by country: http://www.fas.usda.gov/data/cotton-world-markets-and-trade and http://www.fas.usda.gov/psdonline/circulars/cotton.pdf.

26. "GM Cotton's Future in Africa on Shaky Ground," Third World Network Biosafety Information Centre, February 2016, http://www.biosafety-info.net/article.php?aid=1218; Jonathan F. Wendel and Victor A. Albert, "Phylogenetics

of the Cotton Genus," *Systematic Botany* 17, no. 1 (1992), http://www.eeob
.iastate.edu/faculty/WendelJ/pdfs/SystBot1992.pdf; Yousouf Ismael, Richard Ben-
nett, and Stephen Morse, "Benefits from Bt Cotton Use by Smallholder Farmers
in South Africa," AgBioForum (University of Missouri), 2002, http://agbioforum
.org/v5n1/v5n1a01-morse.pdf; Aziz Elbehri and Steve Macdonald, "Estimating
the Impact of Transgenic Bt Cotton on West and Central Africa: A General Equi-
librium Approach," *World Development* 32, no. 12 (2004): 2049–64, http://www
.ask-force.org/web/Cotton/Elbehri-Estimating-Impact-2004.pdf.

27. "Secrets of Lost Empires," *Nova* Online, updated November 2000,
http://www.pbs.org/wgbh/nova/lostempires/china/miracle2.html.

28. Mary Roach, "The Bamboo Solution," *Discover Magazine*, June 1, 1996.

29. Tsuen-hsuin Tsien, *Collected Writings on Chinese Culture* (Hong Kong:
Chinese University Press, 2011).

30. A. F. P. Hulsewé, *Remnants of Ch'in Law: An Annotated Translation of
the Ch'in Legal and Administrative Rules of the 3rd Century BC.* Sinica Leidensia,
No. 17 (Leiden: Brill, 1985).

31. Yang Ye, *Vignettes from the Late Ming: A Hsiao-p'in Anthology* (Seattle:
University of Washington Press, 1999).

32. George B. Kauffman, "Rayon: The First Semi-Synthetic Fiber Product,"
Journal of Chemical Education 70 (1993): 889–93.

33. Anthony Huxley and Mark Griffiths, eds., *The New Royal Horticul-
tural Society Dictionary of Gardening*, June 1999; also Guinness World Records,
http://www.guinnessworldrecords.com/world-records/fastest-growing-plant/.

34. See Worldometers, http://www.worldometers.info/world-population/.

35. Wawan Sujarwo, "Stand Biomass and Carbon Storage of Bamboo Forest
in Penglipuran Traditional Village, Bali (Indonesia)," *Journal of Forestry Research*
27, no. 4 (2016): 913–17.

36. A passenger car emits 9,737.4462 pounds per year, which is 4.41683
metric tons. See "Average Annual Emissions and Fuel Consumption for Gas-
oline-Fueled Passenger Cars and Light Trucks," EPA420-F-08-024, October
2008, https://www3.epa.gov/otaq/consumer/420f08024.pdf.

37. "Four National Retailers Agree to Pay Penalties Totaling $1.26 Million
for Allegedly Falsely Labeling Textiles as Made of Bamboo, While They Actually
Were Rayon," Federal Trade Commission, January 3, 2013, accessed December
13, 2016, https://www.ftc.gov/news-events/press-releases/2013/01/four
-national-retailers-agree-pay-penalties-totaling-126-million.

38. Federal Trade Commission Press Release, "FTC Charges Companies with
'Bamboo-zling' Consumers with False Product Claims," August 11, 2009, https://
www.ftc.gov/news-events/press-releases/2009/08/ftc-charges-companies
-bamboo-zling-consumers-false-product-claims.

39. "FTC Warns 78 Retailers, Including Wal-Mart, Target, and Kmart,
to Stop Labeling and Advertising Rayon Textile Products as 'Bamboo,'"

FTC, February 3, 2010, accessed December 13, 2016, https://www.ftc
.gov/news-events/press-releases/2010/02/ftc-warns-78-retailers-including
-wal-mart-target-kmart-stop.

40. Federal Trade Commission Press Release, "Nordstrom, Bed Bath and
Beyond, Backcountry.com, and JC Penney to Pay Penalties Totaling $1.3 Mil-
lion for Falsely Labeling Rayon Textiles as Made of 'Bamboo,'" December 9,
2015, https://www.ftc.gov/news-events/press-releases/2015/12/nordstrom-bed
-bath-beyond-backcountrycom-jc-penney-pay-penalties.

41. "Not All Bamboo Is Created Equal," Natural Resources Defense
Council, August 2011, https://www.nrdc.org/sites/default/files/CBD_FiberFacts
_Bamboo.pdf.

42. http://www.greenyarn.com/index.htm.

43. Heather Kelly, "Go Offline for 'National Day of Unplugging,'" CNN,
March 6, 2014.

44. Faisal Hoque, "#Unplug: Not What You Think It Is," *Fast Company*,
June 21, 2013, http://www.fastcompany.com/3013212/unplug/unplug-not
-what-you-think-it-is.

45. Baratunde Thurston, "#Unplug: Baratunde Thurston Left the Internet
for 25 Days, and You Should, Too," *Fast Company*, June 17, 2013, http://www
.fastcompany.com/3012521/unplug/baratunde-thurston-leaves-the-internet.

46. Jessica Hullinger, "#Unplug: The Complete, Printable Guide," Fast
Company, June 25, 2013, http://www.fastcompany.com/3012710/unplug/
unplug-the-complete-printable-guide.

47. Rakesh Kochhar, "10 Projections for the Global Population in 2050,"
Pew Research Center, February 3, 2014, http://www.pewresearch.org/fact-tank/
2014/02/03/10-projections-for-the-global-population-in-2050/.

48. Organic Cotton Market Report, Textile Exchange, http://farmhub.tex-
tileexchange.org/farm-library/farm-fiber-reports.

49. Alexander Baier, "Organic Cotton Projects in Africa," PAN Germany,
2005, http://www.pan-germany.org/download/africaprojects.pdf.

50. Syl Tang, "Growing Pains," *Financial Times,* March 2007, http://
hipguide.com/hipprint/pdf/FinancialTimesBusinessofFashion3-3-07Noir.jpg.

51. US Department of Justice, "Armed Conflict Reports: Uganda," https://
www.justice.gov/sites/default/files/eoir/legacy/2014/02/25/Uganda.pdf.

52. The problems continue. A February 2016 audit found that only 46
percent of monies received by the Ministry of Finance were utilized between
January 2013 and June 2015. See The Global Fund, "Global Fund Grants to
the Republic of Uganda," Audit Report GF-OIG-16-005, February 26, 2016,
Full Report http://www.theglobalfund.org/documents/oig/reports/OIG_GF
-OIG-16-005_Report_en/, Summary, http://www.theglobalfund.org/en/oig/
updates/2016-02-26_Audit_of_Global_Fund_Grants_in_Uganda/.

53. Organic Trade Association, "Organic Cotton Facts," http://ota.com/
sites/default/files/indexed_files/OrganicCottonFacts2015.pdf.

54. Gabriel Rangel, with figures by Anna Maurer, "From Corgis to Corn: A Brief Look at the Long History of GMO Technology," *Science in the News* (blog), Harvard University, August 2015 Special Edition, http://sitn.hms.harvard.edu/flash/2015/from-corgis-to-corn-a-brief-look-at-the-long-history-of-gmo-technology/.

55. Amy Harmon, "G.M.O. Myths Spread," *New York Times,* July 12, 2016.

56. *Wikipedia,* s.v. "Farm-to-Table," https://en.wikipedia.org/wiki/Farm-to-table; "What is the Farm-to-Table Movement?"

57. David J. Tenenbaum, "Food vs. Fuel: Diversion of Crops Could Cause More Hunger," Environmental Health Perspectives, National Institutes of Health, June 2008, http://www.ncbi.nlm.nih.gov/pmc/articles/PMC2430252/.

58. Aditya Chakrabortty, "Secret Report: Biofuel Caused Food Crisis," *Guardian,* July 3, 2008, https://www.theguardian.com/environment/2008/jul/03/biofuels.renewableenergy.

59. Timothy A. Wise, "US Corn Ethanol Fuels Food Crisis in Ceveloping Countries," *Al Jazeera,* October 10, 2012, http://www.aljazeera.com/indepth/opinion/2012/10/201210993632838545.html. Timothy A. Wise is the policy research director at the Global Development and Environment Institute, Tufts University.

60. William Pentland, "The Coming Food Crisis: Blame Ethanol?" *Forbes,* July 28, 2012, http://www.forbes.com/sites/williampentland/2012/07/28/the-coming-food-crisis-blame-ethanol/#28efa0eb3ae6.

61. "Zero Hunger," World Food Programme, https://www.wfp.org/hunger/stats.

62. Eleanor Ainge Roy, "Avocado Shortage Fuels Crime Wave in New Zealand," *Guardian,* June 15, 2016, https://www.theguardian.com/world/2016/jun/15/avocado-thieves-shortage-crime-fruit-black-market-new-zealand.

63. Associated Press, "High Avocado Prices Fueling Deforestation," *Register-Guard,* August 14, 2016, http://registerguard.com/rg/business/34673659-63/high-avocado-prices-fueling-deforestation.html.csp.

64. José de Córdoba, "The Violent Gang Wars Behind Your Super Bowl Guacamole," *Wall Street Journal,* January 31, 2014.

65. Susmita Baral, "Are Avocados the New Blood Diamond? Learn the Violent Secret Behind Michoacán's Mexican Avocado Market," *Latin Times,* February 3, 2014, http://www.latintimes.com/are-avocados-new-blood-diamond-learn-violent-secret-behind-michoacans-mexican-avocado-market-149408.

66. Vaclav Smil, *Harvesting the Biosphere: What We Have Taken from Nature* (Cambridge, MA: MIT Press, 2015).

67. Corby Kummer, "Is It Time to Table Farm-to-Table?" *Vanity Fair,* May 18, 2015, http://www.vanityfair.com/culture/2015/05/farm-to-table-what-does-it-mean-anymore.

68. Mark Lynas, "How Land-Inefficient Is Organic Agriculture?" July 16, 2012, http://www.marklynas.org/2012/07/how-land-inefficient-is-organic-agriculture/.

69. Food Standards Agency, "Organic Review Published," July 29, 2009, http://webarchive.nationalarchives.gov.uk/20120206100416/http://food.gov.uk/news/newsarchive/2009/jul/organic.

70. Seanan Forbes, "Foraging Isn't Actually That Cool," *Modern Farmer*, December 15, 2014, http://modernfarmer.com/2014/12/tk-reasons-foraging-sucks/.

71. "Recycled Polyester," Patagonia, https://www.patagonia.com/recycled-polyester.html.

72. "Polartec Celebrates Recycling Its Billionth Plastic Bottle," *Business Wire*, August 5, 2015, http://www.businesswire.com/news/home/20150805005073/en/Polartec-Celebrates-Recycling-Billionth-Plastic-Bottle.

73. "How Much Oil Is Used to Make Plastic?" US Energy Information Administration, last updated April 25, 2016, http://www.eia.gov/tools/faqs/faq.cfm?id=34&t=6.

74. "Natural Gas Explained," US Energy Information Administration, last updated November 21, 2016, http://www.eia.gov/energyexplained/?page=natural_gas_home.

75. I have decided not to take on the countless studies to determine whether or not fracking is detrimental, as it is outside of the bounds of this book. Here is some continued reading: "Natural Gas Extraction: Hydraulic Fracturing," US Environmental Protection Agency, https://www.epa.gov/hydraulicfracturing; "BBC Guide to Fracking," *BBC News*, December 16, 2015, http://www.bbc.com/news/uk-14432401; Mason Inman, "Natural Gas: The Fracking Fallacy," *Nature Magazine*, December 3, 2014, http://www.nature.com/news/natural-gas-the-fracking-fallacy-1.16430; Seamus McGraw, "Is Fracking Safe? The 10 Most Controversial Claims about Natural Gas Drilling," *Popular Mechanics*, May 1, 2016.

76. It is important not to confuse lower gas prices with how much oil we need or consume. Oil prices are low (2014–2016) because of fracking and Iraq stepping up production. More product equals lowered cost, but a current surplus has no bearing on how much we consume annually.

77. "How Much Oil Is Consumed in the United States?" US Energy Information Administration, http://www.eia.gov/tools/faqs/faq.cfm?id=33&t=6.

78. Institute for Energy Research, "U.S. Oil and Gas Production on the Rise Thanks to Fracking," September 19, 2014, http://instituteforenergyresearch.org/analysis/u-s-oil-gas-production-continues-increase-due-hydraulic-fracturing/.

79. "Hydraulic Fracturing Accounts for about Half of Current U.S. Crude Oil Production," US Energy Information Administration, March 15, 2016, http://www.eia.gov/todayinenergy/detail.cfm?id=25372.

80. AirDye is a no-water dyeing process owned by Colorep, a printing and dyeing company that has been a decades-long institution for designers.

Designers who use AirDye include Jeffrey Costello, Robert Tagliapietra, Cynthia Rowley, Miss Peaches Swimwear, Julie Applegate, A Lot to Say, Patagonia, Elaine Ferguson, and Myra Pac.

Chapter 6

1. Syl Tang, "Robots Hit Town," *Financial Times*, January 23, 2005, http://hipguide.com/hipprint/pdf/FinancialTimes1-22-05Robotspage1.jpg.

2. There are a number of sources for this, but I chose the *Guardian* because it mentions her age and professional career: Angelique Chrisafis, "Estelle Balet, Snowboarding Champion, Killed at Age of 21 in Avalanche," *Guardian*, April 19, 2016, https://www.theguardian.com/sport/2016/apr/19/snowboarding-champion-estelle-balet-killed-avalanche.

3. "Matilda Rapaport Dies After Avalanche," *Powder Magazine*, July 18, 2016, http://www.powder.com/stories/matilda-rapaport-dies-avalanche/.

4. American Avalanche Association, "U.S. Avalanche Accidents Report," http://www.avalanche.org/accidents.php; also Jack Lafeman, "NEWS: Worldwide Avalanche Fatalities Up 40% for 2014/2015," October 26, 2015, http://snowbrains.com/avalanche-fatalities-up-40-for-20142015/; also "Utah Avalanche Fatalities in the Modern Era," Utah Avalanche Center, December 10, 2015, https://utahavalanchecenter.org/blog/24973.

5. "How Do People Die When Buried in Avalanche Debris?" Utah Avalanche Center, https://utahavalanchecenter.org/faq. The statistic is also cited here: Jason Blevins, "Colorado Skier Felt Life Fading during 3 Hours Buried in Avalanche," *Denver Post*, April 30, 2016, http://www.denverpost.com/2013/03/30/colorado-skier-felt-life-fading-during-3-hours-buried-in-avalanche/.

6. US Geological Survey, "20 Largest Earthquakes in the World," https://earthquake.usgs.gov/earthquakes/browse/largest-world.php.

7. "Indonesia Quake Toll Jumps Again," *BBC News*, January 25, 2005, http://news.bbc.co.uk/2/hi/asia-pacific/4204385.stm.

8. "Sichuan Earthquake," *New York Times*, http://www.nytimes.com/topic/subject/sichuan-earthquake.

9. There is some dispute over this figure. In 2011, the government had the death toll at 230,000. Therefore 316,000, which is the current official Haitian government number, is controversial. See "Two Years Later, Haitian Earthquake Death Toll in Dispute," *Columbia Journalism Review*, January 12, 2012, http://www.cjr.org/behind_the_news/one_year_later_haitian_earthqu.php. I have cited the official number, but for the purpose of this discussion, it is also not germane.

10. ISECOM, *Hacking Exposed Linux: Linux Security Secrets and Solutions* (New York: McGraw-Hill, 2008), 298; Albert Glinsky, *Theremin: Ether Music and Espionage* (Urbana: University of Illinois Press, 2005).

11. "Ants' Home Search Habit Uncovered," *BBC News*, April 22, 2009, http://news.bbc.co.uk/2/hi/uk_news/england/bristol/somerset/8011998.stm.

12. Paul Miller, "Hitachi's RFID Powder Freaks Us the Heck Out," *Engadget*, February 14, 2007. This was originally written about in Japanese on Sankei Digital: http://www.sankeibiz.jp/.

13. Hsu Chuang Khoo, "Malaysia's Iris May Benefit from U.S. Passport Law," *Yahoo! India News*, May 19 2006, http://archive.li/ukMFM.

14. *Wikipedia*, s.v. "Biometric Passport: Countries Using Biometric Passports," https://en.wikipedia.org/wiki/Biometric_passport.

15. Bob Violino, "RFID in the Global Cattle Industry," *RFID Journal*, July 18, 2004, http://www.rfidjournal.com/articles/view?1034.

16. Thomas C. Greene, "Feds Approve Human RFID Implants," October 14, 2004.

17. Price does not equal distance. A passive tag can go as far up to 10 meters and still be very cheap. It's all the factors combined. See Dipankar Sen, Prosenjit Sen, and Anand M. Das, *RFID for Energy and Utility Industries* (Tulsa, OK: PennWell, 2009), 1–48; Stephen A. Weis, "RFID (Radio Frequency Identification): Principles and Applications," *MIT CSAIL*, 2007, http://www.rfid-off.com/uploads/4/5/1/2/45128343/rfid-article_mit_usa.pdf.

18. "History: Octopus Hong Kong," Octopus, accessed September 9, 2016, http://www.octopus.com.hk/about-us/corporate-profile/our-history/en/index.html.

19. Hong Kong Monetary Authority, "Annual Report 1997," 1997, accessed September 9, 2016, www.hkma.gov.hk/eng/publications-and-research/annual-report/1997.shtml; "Smart Card Case Studies and Implementation Profiles," Smart Card Alliance, December 2003, accessed September 9, 2016, http://www.octopus.com.hk/get-your-octopus/where-can-i-use-it/en/index.html; "Where Can I Use It?" Octopus Hong Kong, accessed September 9, 2016, http://www.octopus.com.hk/get-your-octopus/where-can-i-use-it/en/index.html.

20. Karissa Bell, "This Smart Jacket from Google and Levi's Will Cost You $350," *Mashable*, March 12, 2017, accessed March 13, 2017, http://mashable.com/2017/03/12/google-project-jacquard-levis-jacket-launch.amp?utm.

21. Syl Tang, "Turning Elemental," *Financial Times*, n.d., http://www.ft.com/cms/d31ec170-26a5-11dc-8e18-000b5df10621.html.

22. "Three Out of Five People with Alzheimer's Disease Will Wander," Alzheimer's Association, 2016, accessed September 19, 2016, http://www.alz.org/norcal/in_my_community_18411.asp.

23. Bob DeMarco, "Sobering Statistics about Alzheimer's Wandering," *Alzheimer's Reading Room*, December 19, 2009, http://www.alzheimersreadingroom.com/2009/12/sobering-statistics-about-alzheimers.html.

24. "Aging Statistics," US Department of Health and Human Services, Administration on Aging, May 24, 2016, accessed September 19, 2016, http://www.aoa.acl.gov/Aging_Statistics/index.aspx.

25. "Navlab: The Carnegie Mellon University Navigation Laboratory," The Robotics Institute; "EUREKA Project E!45 PROMETHEUS," EUREKA, accessed September 9, 2016.

26. Mark Green, "Visual Expert Human Factors: Seeing Pedestrians at Night," 2013, accessed September 13, 2016, http://www.visualexpert.com/ Resources/pedestrian.html; Marc Green, Merrill J. Allen, Bernard S. Abrams, Leslie Weintraub, and J. Vernon Odom, *Forensic Vision with Application to Highway Safety* (Tucson, AZ: Lawyers and Judges Publishing Company, 2008).

27. *Wikipedia*, s.v. "City Block," accessed September 13, 2016, https:// en.wikipedia.org/wiki/City_block.

28. "About SmartCap," accessed September 29, 2016, http://www.smart captech.com/about/.

29. Marshall Brain, "How Gyroscopes Work," *How Stuff Works*, April 1, 2000, accessed September 13, 2016, http://science.howstuffworks.com/ gyroscope.htm.

30. Li Ge, Hui Cao, and Raktim Sarma, "Light-Powered Gyroscope Is World's Smallest: Promises a Powerful Spin on Navigation," Optica, accessed September 13, 2016, https://www.eng.yale.edu/caolab/newsbrief/85.pdf.

31. "Cortexica Vision Systems: Visual Search and Image Recognition," 2016, accessed September 13, 2016, https://www.cortexica.com/.

32. Abigail Tucker, "The Freshman at MIT Who Is Revolutionizing Nanotechnology," *Smithsonian Magazine,* December 2013, accessed September 13, 2016, http://www.smithsonianmag.com/innovation/the-freshman-at -mit-who-is-revolutionizing-nanotechnology-180947637/?no-ist.

33. Samsung's S Pen doesn't use GPS technology but something similar.

34. Ludovic Privat, "TI Announced New GPS Chip, Cost Under $5," March 29, 2007, accessed September 15, 2016, http://www.gpsbusinessnews .com/TI-announced-new-GPS-chip-cost-under-5_a102.html.

35. Kelsey D. Atherton, "Put These Quarter-Sized GPS Trackers on Everything," *Popular Science,* October 16, 2013, accessed September 15, 2016, http://www.popsci.com/article/gadgets/put-these-quarter-sized-gps-trackers -everything.

36. Katherine Boehret, "TrackR Vs. Tile: The Lost-and-Found Face-Off," *ReCode,* April 1, 2015, accessed September 15, 2016, http://www.recode .net/2015/4/1/11560992/trackr-vs-tile-the-lost-and-found-face-off.

37. "Blog Archives: Energy Floors," August 31, 2016, accessed September 19, 2016, http://www.energy-floors.com/category/blog/.

38. SnowBrains, "Brain Post: How Far Does the Average Human Walk in a Lifetime?" July 2, 2015, accessed September 19, 2016, http://snowbrains.com/ brain-post-how-far-does-the-average-human-walk-in-a-lifetime/.

39. Larissa Danielle Green, Jessica Gross, and Kate Torgovnick, "Energy from Your Feet: When Sidewalks and Dance Floors Become Energy Sources,"

TED, June 3, 2013, accessed September 19, 2016, http://blog.ted.com/energy
-from-your-feet-when-sidewalks-and-dance-floors-become-energy-sources/.

40. Pavegen Case Studies, April 27, 2016, accessed September 19, 2016,
http://www.pavegen.com/permanent/.

41. Ellie Zolfagharifard, "Flexible Material Can Charge Devices While You
Move," *Daily Mail,* February 25, 2014, http://www.dailymail.co.uk/sciencetech/
article-2567449/Forget-chargers-soon-use-CARPETS-power-phones-Fibre
-harnesses-solar-energy-footsteps-generate-electricity.html.

42. "EPGLMed Homepage," 2016, accessed September 19, 2016, http://
www.epglmed.com/.

43. David Shamah, "World's Smallest GPS Chip Makes Wearables More
Wearable," *Times of Israel,* September 5, 2014, http://www.timesofisrael.com/
worlds-smallest-gps-chip-makes-wearables-more-wearable/.

44. Paolo Magrassi, "Why a Universal RFID Infrastructure Would Be a
Good Thing," Gartner research report G00106518, May 2, 2002, https://www
.gartner.com/doc/356347/universal-rfid-infrastructure-good-thing.

45. Junko Yoshida, "German 'Smart' Supermarket Rolls RFID System," *EE
Times,* May 5, 2003, accessed September 19, 2016, http://www.eetimes.com/
document.asp?doc_id=1146015.

46. "The 2013 National Supermarket Shrink Survey," accessed September
19, 2016, http://www.theshrinksurvey.com/.

47. Syl Tang, "Going Back on Returns?" *Financial Times,* February 25, 2006,
http://www.ft.com/cms/s/0/cb1edcce-a5a2-11da-bf34-0000779e2340.html.

48. Talk given at Bryant Park Grill for the Ad Club of New York.

49. Charles Duhigg, "How Companies Learn Your Secrets," *New York Times
Magazine,* January 1, 2016, http://www.nytimes.com/2012/02/19/magazine/
shopping-habits.html.

50. Ann-Christine Diaz, "Facial Recognition Technology Makes Marketers
a Fun Big Brother," *AdAge,* September 18, 2013, accessed September 19, 2016,
http://adage.com/article/news/brands-facial-recognition-campaigns/244233/.

51. Jessica Davies, "How BBC Uses Facial Recognition to Measure Native
Advertising," *Digiday,* January 21, 2016, accessed September 19, 2016, http://
digiday.com/publishers/bbc-facial-recognition-native-advertising/.

52. Sean Hargrave, "Facial Recognition—a Powerful Ad Tool or Privacy
Nightmare?" *Guardian,* August 17, 2016, https://www.theguardian.com/media
-network/2016/aug/17/facial-recognition-a-powerful-ad-tool-or-privacy-nightmare.

53. "*Innerspace* (1987)," IMDb, http://www.imdb.com/title/tt0093260/.

54. Nikolay Nikolov, "These Tattoos Conduct Electricity, Turning You into a
Very Basic Cyborg," *Mashable,* March 6, 2017, accessed March 13, 2017, http://
mashable.com/2017/03/06/electroconductive-ink-tattoo-monitor-health/.

55. Kristine Johnson, "Seen at 11: These Microchips Are Implanted into
Your Hand to Replace Keys, Passwords," *CBS New York,* July 29, 2016, accessed
March 13, 2017, http://newyork.cbslocal.com/2016/07/29/hand-microchips/.

56. Syl Tang, "The Next Frontier: If Apple Comes In, It Is Sure to Change the Game," *Financial Times*, June 8, 2013, https://www.ft.com/content/ba13e4f8-a52f-11e2-8777-00144feabdc0.

57. Syl Tang, "Olympic Sponsors Swatch and Visa Get Set to Compete with Apple," *Financial Times*, January 17, 2016, https://www.ft.com/content/a6a5df00-9d09-11e5-8ce1-f6219b685d74.

58. The watch sold for 580 yuan in China (around eighty-seven dollars, at the time of the writing of this book).

59. *Wikipedia*, s.v. "List of Earthquakes in India," accessed September 21, 2016, https://en.wikipedia.org/wiki/List_of_earthquakes_in_India.

Chapter 7

1. "Liquids Rule," Transportation Security Administration, accessed October 17, 2016, https://www.tsa.gov/travel/security-screening/liquids-rule.

2. "TSA Will Allow Small Knives on Planes Again," March 5, 2013, accessed October 17, 2016, https://www.knife-depot.com/blog/tsa-will-allow-small-knives-on-planes-again/.

3. Daniel Lawton, "TSA's Pocket Knife Ban: The Blow-by-Blow," May 13, 2013, accessed October 17, 2016, https://www.knife-depot.com/blog/will-pocket-knives-be-allowed-on-planes/.

4. Lisa Stark, "TSA Fires Hundreds of Airport Screeners," *ABC News*, January 7, 2006, accessed October 17, 2016, http://abcnews.go.com/WNT/story?id=129658&page=1.

5. Congresswoman Marsha Blackburn, "Not on My Watch: 50 Failures of TSA's Transportation Security Officers," US House of Representatives, 112th Congress, accessed October 17, 2016, http://blackburn.house.gov/uploadedfiles/blackburn_tso_report.pdf.

6. Bianca Posterli, "Snuggle Up with a Sleeping Bag Coat." *The Frisky,* October 31, 2009, accessed October 17, 2016, http://www.thefrisky.com/2009-10-31/snuggle-with-norma-kamali/; Mary Hall, "Norma Kamali Sleeping Bag Coat Now Online at Walmart.com," *Recessionista,* October 29, 2009, accessed October 17, 2016, http://therecessionista.com/norma-kamali-sleeping-bag-coat-now/.

7. Syl Tang, "Not Too Much to Declare," *Financial Times*, September 2, 2006, http://www.ft.com/cms/s/0/282f21d2-3a20-11db-90bb-0000779e2340.html.

8. Samuel P. Huntington, "The Clash of Civilizations?" *Foreign Affairs*, Summer 1993, https://www.foreignaffairs.com/articles/united-states/1993-06-01/clash-civilizations.

9. Jonathan B. Freeman, Andrew M. Penner, Aliya Saperstein, Matthias Scheutz, and Nalini Ambady, "Looking the Part: Social Status Cues Shape

Race Perception," *PLOS ONE Journal*, September 26, 2011, http://dx.doi.org/ 10.1371/journal.pone.0025107. This study is also available through the National Institutes of Health.

10. Hayley Phelan, "How Personal Style Bloggers Are Raking in Millions," *Fashionista*, August 20, 2013, http://fashionista.com/2013/08/how-personal -style-bloggers-are-raking-in-millions#1.

11. Meghan Blalock, "You Won't Believe How Much Money *The Blonde Salad* Will Make This Year," *Who What Wear,* September 9, 2014, accessed October 17, 2016, http://www.whowhatwear.com/the-blonde-salad-millions.

12. "LIKEtoKNOW.it," accessed October 17, 2016, http://liketoknow .it; "Have2Have.It," accessed October 17, 2016, https://have2have.it/; Carlina Harris, "Introducing Emoticode, the Newest Way to Monetize Your Snapchat," June 2, 2016, accessed October 17, 2016, http://blog.shopstyle collective.com/2016/06/02/introducing-emoticode-the-newest-way-to -monetize-your-snapchat/.

13. Lucy Pavia, "Kardashian Net Worth: How Much Money Do They All Have Individually?" *InStyle Magazine,* August 10, 2016, accessed October 18, 2016, http://www.instyle.co.uk/celebrity/news/the-kardashian-rich -list-what-are-they-all-worth-individually.

14. Tony Maglio, Greg Gilman, Matt Donnelly, Alicia Banks, and Debbie Emery, "'Keeping Up with the Kardashians' Premiere Down from Last Season's Debut," *The Wrap,* March 17, 2015, accessed October 18, 2016, http://www .thewrap.com/keeping-up-with-the-kardashians-season-10-premiere-the-royals -tv-ratings-viewers-e/.

15. "Exposure Without Disclosure: Cashing in with the Kardashians," *Truth in Advertising,* August 22, 2016, accessed October 18, 2016, https://www .truthinadvertising.org/exposure-without-disclosure-cashing-kardashians/.

16. Angelique Chrisafis, "French Pool Bans 'Burkini' Swim," *BBC News*, August 12, 2009, http://news.bbc.co.uk/2/hi/europe/8197917.stm.

17. Reuters, "French Driver Is Fined for Wearing a Veil," *New York Times*, April 23, 2010, http://www.nytimes.com/2010/04/24/world/europe/24france.html.

18. "Driver Wearing Islamic Face Veil Fined in France," *CNSN,* April 23, 2010, accessed October 18, 2016, http://cnsnews.com/news/article/ driver-wearing-islamic-face-veil-fined-france.

19. Edward Cody, "France Moves to Fine Muslim Women with Full-Face Islamic Veils," *Washington Post,* May 20, 2010, http://www.washingtonpost .com/wp-dyn/content/article/2010/05/19/AR2010051901653.html?nav =emailpage&tid=a_inl; Max Colchester, "French Veil Ban Takes Effect," *Wall Street Journal,* April 11, 2011, accessed March 13, 2017, https://www.wsj.com/ articles/SB10001424052748704662604576256493482608356; "2 Arrested as France's Ban on Burqas, Niqabs Takes Effect," *CNN.com,* April 12, 2011, accessed March 13, 2017, http://www.cnn.com/2011/WORLD/europe/04/11/ france.burqa.ban/.

20. Edward Cody, "Tensions Flare in France over Veil Ban," *Washington Post*, August 9, 2012, https://www.washingtonpost.com/world/tensions-flare-in-france-over-veil-ban/2012/08/08/67b56fc2-e150-11e1-98e7-89d659f9c106_story.html.

21. "Driver Wearing Islamic Face Veil Fined."

22. Andrew Bowen, "Spanish Senate Narrowly Votes to Support Ban of Islamic Body Veil," *Deutsche Welle*, June 23, 2010, http://www.dw.com/en/spanish-senate-narrowly-votes-to-support-ban-of-islamic-body-veil/a-5724242.

23. Michael Lipka and Conrad Hackett, "Why Muslims Are the World's Fastest-Growing Religious Group," Pew Research Center, April 23, 2015, accessed October 18, 2016, http://www.pewresearch.org/fact-tank/2015/04/23/why-muslims-are-the-worlds-fastest-growing-religious-group/.

24. Hijab: scarf covering head and neck but not face. Burkini: full body swimsuit leaving face, hands, and feet uncovered. Burqa: full body garment with mesh over the eyes. Niqab: full face veil that exposes only the eyes.

25. Angelique Chrisafis, "French Mayors Refuse to Lift Burkini Ban Despite Court Ruling," *Guardian*, August 29, 2016, https://www.theguardian.com/world/2016/aug/28/french-mayors-burkini-ban-court-ruling.

26. *Wikipedia*, s.v. "Brigitte Bardot," accessed October 18, 2016, https://en.wikipedia.org/wiki/Brigitte_Bardot.

27. *Wikipedia*, s.v. "Roger Vadim," accessed October 18, 2016, https://en.wikipedia.org/wiki/Roger_Vadim.

28. Jacques-Albin-Simon Collin de Plancy, *Dictionnaire Infernal, Ou, Recherches Et Anecdotes . . .* , Volumes 1–2 (n.p.: Fain, 1818); *Wikipedia*, s.v. "Belphegor," accessed October 18, 2016, https://en.wikipedia.org/wiki/Belphegor; Kalhmah, "Dictionnaire Infernal: Romans Nouvelle et Theatre," *La Horde Noire*, 2002, accessed October 18, 2016, http://www.lahordenoire-metalcom/lettre-noire/roman-nouvelle-theatre/dictionnaire-infernal.html.

29. "Le Mot du Maire: Ville du Touquet-Paris-Plage," 2016, accessed October 18, 2016, http://www.lestouquettois.fr/la-mairie/le-mot-du-maire.html.

30. Alissa J. Rubin, "Fighting for the 'Soul of France,' More Towns Ban a Bathing Suit: The Burkini," *New York Times*, August 23, 2016, http://www.nytimes.com/2016/08/18/world/europe/fighting-for-the-soul-of-france-more-towns-ban-a-bathing-suit-the-burkini.html.

31. Ibid.

32. Alissa J. Rubin, "French 'Burkini' Bans Provoke Backlash as Armed Police Confront Beachgoers," *New York Times*, August 26, 2016, http://www.nytimes.com/2016/08/25/world/europe/france-burkini.html.

33. It is from the French constitution, Article 1, which states that France is a secular republic ("La France est une République indivisible, laïque, démocratique et sociale"). Many scholars contend there is no direct translation from French. As a fluent French speaker, I am inclined to agree, but here is a fairly

good summarization, "The Concept of *laïcité* in France," Normandy Vision, accessed October 18, 2016, http://www.normandyvision.org/article12030701.php.

34. "The Mezuzah Throughout the Ages," *ajudaicablog*, December 20, 2012, accessed October 18, 2016, http://blog.ajudaica.com/2012/12/the-mezuzah-throughout-the-ages/.

35. Adam Withnall and John Lichfield, "Charlie Hebdo Shooting: At Least 12 Killed as Shots Fired at Satirical Magazine's Paris Office," *Independent–Europe*, January 7, 2015, http://www.independent.co.uk/news/world/europe/charlie-hebdo-shooting-10-killed-as-shots-fired-at-satirical-magazine-headquarters-according-to-9962337.html.

36. *Wikipedia*, s.v. "Porte de Vincennes Siege," accessed October 18, 2016, https://en.wikipedia.org/wiki/Porte_de_Vincennes_siege.

37. Eleanor Steafel, "Paris Terror Attack: Everything We Know on Saturday Afternoon," *Telegraph*, November 21, 2015, http://www.telegraph.co.uk/news/worldnews/europe/france/11995246/Paris-shooting-What-we-know-so-far.html.

38. Chris Stephen, "Nice Attack Bewilders Mohamed Lahouaiej-Bouhlel's Relatives," *Guardian*, July 16, 2016, https://www.theguardian.com/world/2016/jul/16/nice-attack-bewilders-mohamed-lahouaiej-bouhlel-relatives; Peter Beaumont and Sofia Fischer, "Mohamed Lahouaiej-Bouhlel: Who was the Bastille Day Truck Attacker?" *Guardian*, July 16, 2016, https://www.theguardian.com/world/2016/jul/15/bastille-day-truck-driver-was-known-to-police-reports-say.

39. *Wikipedia*, s.v. "Omar Mateen," accessed October 18, 2016, https://en.wikipedia.org/wiki/Omar_Mateen; *Wikipedia*, s.v. "Rizwan Farook and Tashfeen Malik," accessed October 18, 2016, https://en.wikipedia.org/wiki/Rizwan_Farook_and_Tashfeen_Malik.

40. Angelique Chrisafis, "French Mayors Refuse to Lift Burkini Ban Despite Court Ruling," *Guardian*, August 29, 2016, https://www.theguardian.com/world/2016/aug/28/french-mayors-burkini-ban-court-ruling.

41. In and of itself, an interesting example of people using clothes quite specifically to signal their threatening nature—red and blue gang colors. Many of what are now thought of as hip-hop fashion staples arose for practical reasons in gang combat—bandanas for demonstrating membership, puffy coats and baggy jeans for concealing firearms, etc.

42. *Crips and Bloods: Made in America*, Independent Lens (PBS), 2015, accessed October 18, 2016, http://www.pbs.org/independentlens/cripsandbloods/film.html.

43. Centers for Disease Control and Prevention, "Impaired Driving: Get the Facts," April 15, 2016, accessed October 18, 2016, http://www.cdc.gov/motorvehiclesafety/impaired_driving/impaired-drv_factsheet.html.

44. Centers for Disease Control and Prevention, "Unintentional Drowning: Get the Facts," April 28, 2016, accessed October 18, 2016, http://www.cdc.gov/homeandrecreationalsafety/water-safety/waterinjuries-factsheet.html.

45. The figure is valid at the time of the writing of this book. See Karen Yourish et al., "How Many People Have Been Killed in ISIS Attacks Around the World," *New York Times*, July 16, 2016, http://www.nytimes.com/interactive/2016/03/25/world/map-isis-attacks-around-the-world.html?_r=0; "How Many People Have Been Killed by ISIS?" accessed October 18, 2016, https://www.quora.com/How-many-people-have-been-killed-by-ISIS.

46. The number varies. The UN says 400,000 (March 15, 2011–April 23, 2016) and is quoted here: "Syria Death Toll: UN Envoy Estimates 400,000 Killed," *Aljazeera.com*, April 23, 2016, accessed March 13, 2017, http://www.aljazeera.com/news/2016/04/staffan-de-mistura-400000-killed-syria-civil-war-160423055735629.html. The Syrian Center for Policy Research says 470,000 (March 15, 2011–February 11, 2016) and is quoted here: Priyanka Boghani, "A Staggering New Death Toll for Syria's War—470,000," *Frontline*, February 11, 2016, accessed March 13, 2017, http://www.pbs.org/wgbh/frontline/article/a-staggering-new-death-toll-for-syrias-war-470000/.

47. National Sex Offender Public Website (NSOPW), US Department of Justice, "Facts and Statistics," December 5, 2012, accessed October 19, 2016, https://www.nsopw.gov/en-us/Education/FactsStatistics.

48. Terri Peters, "How the 'Tricky People' Concept Teaches Kids to Spot Unsafe Adults," *TODAY*, June 7, 2016, http://www.today.com/parents/forget-stranger-danger-tricky-people-concept-helps-kids-spot-sketchy-t95021; "'Tricky' People Are the New Strangers," *CBS*, June 27, 2012, http://miami.cbslocal.com/2012/06/27/tricky-people-are-the-new-strangers/; Adam Carter, "Is 'Tricky People' the New 'Don't Talk to Strangers' for Kids?," *CBC News*, September 2, 2015, accessed October 19, 2016, http://www.cbc.ca/news/canada/hamilton/news/is-tricky-people-the-new-don-t-talk-to-strangers-for-kids-1.3211997.

49. French version, Michel Houellebecq, *Sumision* (Anagrama, 2015); English version, Michel Houellebecq, *Submission* (Farrar Straus Giroux, 2015).

50. Lydia Kiesling, "The Elegant Bigotry of Michel Houellebecq's *Submission*." *Slate.com*, October 6, 2015, accessed October 23, 2016, http://www.slate.com/articles/arts/books/2015/10/submission_by_michel_houellebecq_reviewed.html; Heller McAlpin, "Don't Take 'Submission' Lying Down," *NPR*, October 20, 2015, accessed October 23, 2016, http://www.npr.org/2015/10/20/448977012/dont-take-submission-lying-down; Alex Preston, "*Submission* by Michel Houellebecq Review: Satire That's More Subtle Than It Seems," *Guardian*, September 8, 2015, https://www.theguardian.com/books/2015/sep/08/submission-michel-houellebecq-review-satire-islamic-france; Karl Ove Knausgaard, "Michel Houellebecq's 'Submission'," *New York Times Sunday Book Review*, November 2, 2015, http://www.nytimes.com/2015/11/08/books/review/michel-houellebecqs-submission.html?_r=0.

51. "What Is the Meaning of the Word 'Islam'?" *Muslim Voices*, October 1, 2008, accessed October 23, 2016, http://muslimvoices.org/word-islam-meaning/.

52. *Wikipedia*, s.v. "Dinesh D'Souza," accessed October 23, 2016, https://en.wikipedia.org/wiki/Dinesh_D%27Souza; *Wikipedia*, s.v. "Norman Podhoretz," accessed October 23, 2016, https://en.wikipedia.org/wiki/Norman_Podhoretz.

53. Ruth Sherlock, Joe Daunt, and Sam Tarling, "Found: The Bethnal Green Schoolgirls Who Ran Away to Syria," *Telegraph*, July 3, 2015, http://www.telegraph.co.uk/news/2016/03/18/found-the-bethnal-green-schoolgirls-who-ran-away-to-syria/.

54. Aurelien Breeden and Lilia Blaise, "Court Overturns 'Burkini' Ban in French Town," *New York Times,* September 9, 2016, http://www.nytimes.com/2016/08/27/world/europe/france-burkini-ban.html.

55. Kristina Rizga, Andrew Bacevich, Edwin Rios, David Corn, Alexander Sammon, and Hannah Levintova, "This Is What It's Like to Be a Muslim Schoolkid in America Right Now," *Mother Jones*, December 9, 2015, accessed October 19, 2016, http://www.motherjones.com/politics/2015/12/muslim-kids-bullying-schools-teachers-islamophobia.

56. Jill Tucker, "Study Finds Majority of Muslims Have Faced Bullying at School," *San Francisco Chronicle,* October 30, 2015, accessed October 19, 2016, http://www.sfchronicle.com/education/article/With-education-and-humor-taking-aim-at-bullying-6601785.php.

57. "Executive Order: Protecting the Nation from Foreign Terrorist Entry into the United States," Whitehouse.gov, January 27, 2017, accessed March 13, 2017, https://www.whitehouse.gov/the-press-office/2017/01/27/executive-order-protecting-nation-foreign-terrorist-entry-united-states.

58. Uri Friedman, "Where America's Terrorists Actually Come From," *Atlantic*, January 30, 2017, accessed March 13, 2017, https://www.theatlantic.com/international/archive/2017/01/trump-immigration-ban-terrorism/514361.

59. Alex Nowrasteh, "Terrorism and Immigration: A Risk Analysis," Cato Institute, September 13, 2016, accessed March 13, 2017, https://www.cato.org/publications/policy-analysis/terrorism-immigration-risk-analysis.

60. Ghazala Irshad, "How Anti-Muslim Sentiment Plays out in Classrooms Across the US," *Guardian*, January 5, 2016, https://www.theguardian.com/us-news/2015/dec/21/anti-muslim-harassment-american-classrooms-student-bullying.

61. Nico Hines, "Ibtihaj Muhammad, Hijab-Wearing Olympic Star: I'm Not Safe in the U.S.," *Daily Beast,* August 4, 2016, accessed October 23, 2016, http://www.thedailybeast.com/articles/2016/08/04/ibtihaj-muhammad-hijab-wearing-olympic-star-i-m-not-safe-in-the-u-s.html.

62. "Qandeel Baloch: Pakistan Social Media Celebrity 'Killed by Brother,'" *BBC News*, July 16, 2016, http://www.bbc.com/news/world-asia-36814258.

63. Marissa Wenzke, "A Saudi YouTube Star Was Arrested over His 'enticing' Video Chats," *Mashable*, September 28, 2016, http://mashable.com/2016/09/28/saudi-teen-in-jail-for-chat-videos/#_okX6.sJLaqN; "The Saudi Teen Arrested for Flirting Online," *BBC Magazine*, n.d., http://www.bbc.com/

news/magazine-37683947; Samuel Osborne, "Saudi Arabian Teenage YouTube Star Arrested over 'Enticing' Videos with Female American Blogger 'Repents,'" *Independent–Middle East*, October 11, 2016, http://www.independent.co.uk/news/world/middle-east/saudi-arabia-abu-sin-arrested-christina-crockett-teenage-youtube-younow-videos-repents-a7356011.html.

64. Palash Ghosh, "Bollywood at 100: How Big Is India's Mammoth Film Industry?" *International Business Times*, May 3, 2013, http://www.ibtimes.com/bollywood-100-how-big-indias-mammoth-film-industry-1236299.

65. "Bollywood's Expanding Reach," *BBC News*, May 3, 2012, http://www.bbc.com/news/world-asia-india-17920845; Andrew Leonard, "Bollywood in Africa—Is It Getting Too Western?" *Salon,* June 13, 2007, http://www.salon.com/2007/06/13/bollywood_in_africa/; Ada Lio, "Baz Luhrmann Interview on *Moulin Rouge!*" About.com, http://movies.about.com/library/weekly/aa030902a.htm.

66. "Deepika Padukone Is World's 10th Highest Paid Actress, Beats Priyanka Chopra to *Forbes* List," *Indian Express*, August 25, 2016, accessed October 20, 2016, http://indianexpress.com/article/entertainment/bollywood/deepika-padukone-jennifer-lawrence-priyanka-chopra-forbes-100-highest-paid-actress-list-2993661/.

67. *Wikipedia*, s.v. "Bollywood," accessed October 23, 2016, https://en.wikipedia.org/wiki/Bollywood#Genre_conventions.

68. Prashant Singh, "What's the Big Deal about a Kiss, Asks Bollywood," *Hindustan Times, New Delhi*, August 25, 2014, accessed October 23, 2016, http://www.hindustantimes.com/bollywood/what-s-the-big-deal-about-a-kiss-asks-bollywood/story-GcUnU5O5nzolVflCfo0aYP.html.

69. "How the 'Good Hindu Girl' Dresses: The Role of Modesty in Female Clothing." *sword + flute*, April 17, 2013, accessed October 20, 2016, https://swordandflute.wordpress.com/2013/04/17/how-the-good-hindu-girl-dresses-the-role-of-modesty-in-female-clothing/.

70. Shaan Khan, "What's Really Behind India's Rape Crisis," *Daily Beast,* March 25, 2016, accessed October 20, 2016, http://www.thedailybeast.com/articles/2016/03/25/what-s-really-behind-india-s-rape-crisis.html.

71. "Dressing the Indian Woman Through History," *BBC Magazine*, December 6, 2014, http://www.bbc.com/news/magazine-30330693.

72. Khan, "What's Really Behind India's Rape Crisis."

73. Juliet Perry and Sugam Pokharel, "14-Year-Old Girl Dies in Second Shocking Double Rape Case in India," *CNN*, July 26, 2016, http://www.cnn.com/2016/07/26/asia/india-rape-cases/.

74. Nitasha Natu, "Actor Gauhar Khan Slapped for 'Skimpy' Dress." *Times of India,* December 1, 2014, http://timesofindia.indiatimes.com/india/Actor-Gauhar-Khan-slapped-for-skimpy-dress/articleshow/45329277.cms.

75. Angelique Chrisafis, "French Mayors Refuse to Lift Burkini Ban Despite Court Ruling," *Guardian*, August 29, 2016, https://www.theguardian.com/world/2016/aug/28/french-mayors-burkini-ban-court-ruling.

76. David Chazan, "French Mayors Who Banned Burkini to Defy Court Ruling Against Them," *Telegraph*, August 28, 2016, http://www.telegraph.co.uk/news/2016/08/28/french-towns-who-banned-burkini-to-defy-court-ruling-against-the/.

77. L. R. Williams, "Beliefs and Attitudes of Young Girls Regarding Menstruation," in *Menarche*, ed. Sharon Golub (Lexington, MA: Lexington Books, 1983), 139–48; S. Laws, *Issues of Blood: The Politics of Menstruation* (London: Macmillan, 1980).

78. T. Buckley and A. Gottlieb, eds., *Blood Magic: The Anthropology of Menstruation* (Berkeley: University of California Press, 1988).

79. Romil Patel, "Nude Selfies: The Latest Trend Sweeping the Millennials—but There's a Cost," *International Business Times*, March 5, 2016, http://www.ibtimes.co.uk/nude-selfies-latest-trend-sweeping-millennials-theres-cost-1547667.

80. "Half of Millennials Admit They Have Texted Naked Pictures," *Daily Mail*, September 8, 2015, http://www.dailymail.co.uk/femail/article-3225666/HALF-millennials-admit-sent-naked-pictures-text-quarter-say-rely-online-dating-sites-love.html.

81. Bobbi Rebell, "For Millennials, Going Naked Online Better Than Data Breach," *Reuters*, July 9, 2015, accessed October 19, 2016, http://www.reuters.com/article/us-column-rebell-naked-idUSKCN0PJ2C620150709.

82. Peggy Orenstein, *Girls and Sex* (New York: Harper, 2016), https://www.harpercollins.com/9780062209726/girls-and-sex; Cindi Leive, "Sext and the Single Girl," *New York Times Book Reviews*, March 23, 2016, http://www.nytimes.com/2016/03/27/books/review/sext-and-the-single-girl.html; "'Girls and Sex' and the Importance of Talking to Young Women about Pleasure," *NPR*, March 29, 2016, accessed October 23, 2016, http://www.npr.org/sections/health-shots/2016/03/29/472211301/girls-sex-and-the-importance-of-talking-to-young-women-about-pleasure; Nancy Jo Sales, *American Girls: Social Media and the Secret Lives of Teenagers* (New York: Knopf, 2016), https://www.amazon.com/American-Girls-Social-Secret-Teenagers/dp/0385353928; Anna North, "'American Girls,' by Nancy Jo Sales," *New York Times Book Reviews*, March 25, 2016, http://www.nytimes.com/2016/03/27/books/review/american-girls-by-nancy-jo-sales.html.

83. Sarah A. Petersen, "Jewish Woman Launches Modest Online Marketplace for Women Around the World," *Deseret News*, February 27, 2015, http://www.deseretnews.com/article/865622949/Jewish-woman-says-modesty-spans-religions-and-cultures-launches-modest-online-marketplace.html?pg=all.

84. Antonia Mortensen and Angela Dewan, "French Towns Maintain Burkini Bans Despite Court Rulings," *CNN*, August 31, 2016, http://www.cnn.com/2016/08/31/europe/france-burkini-ban/.

85. Lorraine Ali, "For American Muslims, Choosing to Wear the Veil Poses Challenges," *New York Times*, September 30, 2014, http://www.nytimes.com/2010/06/13/fashion/13veil.html.

86. Sarah Kaplan, "Meet Ibtihaj Muhammad, the History-Making Olympian Who Called out SXSW for Telling Her to Remove Her Hijab," *Washington Post*, March 14, 2016, https://www.washingtonpost.com/news/morning-mix/wp/2016/03/14/meet-ibtihaj-muhammad-the-history-making-olympian-who-called-out-sxsw-for-telling-her-to-remove-her-hijab/.

87. Rose Minutaglio, "Ibtihaj Muhammad to Compete in Olympics Wearing Hijab," *People,* July 28, 2016, accessed October 23, 2016, http://people.com/sports/ibtihaj-muhammad-to-compete-in-olympics-wearing-hijab/; J. Weston Phippen, "An American Hijab at the Olympics," *Atlantic*, February 4, 2016, accessed October 23, 2016, http://www.theatlantic.com/national/archive/2016/02/first-olympic-athlete-in-hijab/459933/; Nicholas Hautman, "First U.S. Olympian to Compete in Hijab Wins Bronze Medal," *US Weekly,* August 13, 2016, accessed October 23, 2016, http://www.usmagazine.com/celebrity-news/news/ibtihaj-muhammad-first-us-olympian-to-compete-in-hijab-wins-bronze-w434371; Dan Wolken, "Ibtihaj Muhammad Makes U.S. History, Wears Hijab in Olympics," *USA Today*, August 8, 2016, http://www.usatoday.com/story/sports/olympics/2016/08/08/ibtihaj-muhammad-makes-us-history-wears-hijab-in-olympics/88399686/.

88. Ghazala Khan, "Ghazala Khan: Trump Criticized My Silence. He Knows Nothing about True Sacrifice," *Washington Post*, July 31, 2016, https://www.washingtonpost.com/opinions/ghazala-khan-donald-trump-criticized-my-silence-he-knows-nothing-about-true-sacrifice/2016/07/31/c46e52ec-571c-11e6-831d-0324760ca856_story.html?utm_term=.0a3d915b254c.

89. Aysha Khan, "Nike to Launch 'Pro Hijab' for Muslim Women Athletes," *USA Today*, March 7, 2017, accessed March 13, 2017, http://www.usatoday.com/story/sports/2017/03/07/nike-pro-hijab-muslim-women-athletes/98874526/.

90. Douglas Robson, "In Early Rounds at French Open, Turkish Tennis Player Makes History," *Washington Post*, May 24, 2016, accessed March 13, 2017, https://www.washingtonpost.com/sports/tennis/in-early-rounds-at-french-open-turkish-tennis-player-makes-history/2016/05/24/d3019d7a-21d2-11e6-aa84-42391ba52c91_story.html?utm_term=.dfe29bc8576f.

91. *Wikipedia*, s.v. "Aravane Rezaï," accessed March 13, 2017, https://en.wikipedia.org/wiki/Aravane_Reza%C3%AF.

92. Sheena McKenzie, "French Mayors Maintain Burkini Bans Despite Court Ruling," *CNN*, August 29, 2016, http://www.cnn.com/2016/08/29/europe/french-mayors-refuse-lift-burkini-ban/.

Conclusion

1. George Nolfi, *The Adjustment Bureau*, Universal Pictures, 2011.

2. Alexander Fury, "Can a Corset Be Feminist?" *New York Times*, December 1, 2016, http://www.nytimes.com/2016/11/25/t-magazine/fashion/corset-history -feminism.html.

3. Ginia Bellafante, "Your Public Service Ad? Not Here," *New York Times*, October 20, 2016, http://www.nytimes.com/2016/10/09/nyregion/your-public -service-ad-not-here.html.

INDEX

burkini: culture and, 106–7; French ban of, 107–8; *laïcité* and, 108; war of, 117

Burroughs, William, 27

Calvin Klein, x

Camping, Harold, 5

Chanel, xii

Charlie Hebdo, 109

charms, 5

Chilton, Nancy, 25

China: Apple and, 64; consumption and, 65–66; economy of, 64

Christie's auction house, 17, 19–20, 23

circular economy, 63

civilizations, 103–4

Claw Money, x

clothes-laundering: Kennedy and, 38; in marriage, 121; Upper East Side and, 38

clothing: agriculture and, 73; beliefs through, 15; changing world with, 52–53; civilizations clash with, 103–4; cultural war with, 117; for culture, 104; eBay recycling with, 58; eco-friendly and, 76; human need and, 10; industry of, 53, 81; Islamophobia and, 111; memory and, 12; old man chic as, 12; perception through, 10, 120; photo voltaic-piezoelectric and, 96; pollution and, 53; with recycling, 42–43; RFID and, 87, 91; safety through, 91; trends of, ix; TSA and, 103–4; utility for, 90; world reflecting with, 1. *See also* cycling-clothing; fake clothing; fashion industry; knockoff clothing; utilitarian clothing; wearables

cold reading, 10

Comic-Con, xi

confirmation bias, 27, 33

connected homes, 97

consumer culture, 65, 76

consumers: China and, 64; couponing and, 60–61; Freemeets consumption for, 56; perception of, 60

consumption: China and, 65–66; household income and, 66; for planet Earth, 82

contactless verification, 89

coral reefs, 55. *See also* runoffs

Costume Institute, 24

cotton: Africa industry of, 74; industry of, 73; pollution and, 73. *See also* organic cotton

counterfeit denim, 30

Counterfeiting Luxury, 31

couponing, 60–61

culture: Arab Spring and, 106–7; burkini and, 106–7; clothing for, 104; France and, 106–7; future problems for, 104–5; honor killing and, 113; Muslims and, 112; as new war, 105–6; perception and, 114; rape and, 114–15

cyanide fishing, 55

cycling-clothing, 39–40

Dahan, Jerome, 30

Damasio, Antonio, 8

Damisch, Lysann, 6

Dayton, George, 59

decision-making, 8

declarative memory, 13

The Devil Wears Prada, xiii, 96

Diouf, Jacques, 80

divorce, 46–49

Easton, Simon, 23–24
eBay, 58
eco-friendly, 76
economics, 45
Economist, x
economy: of China, 64; circular, 63; clothing industry and, 81; cycle of, 65; divorce and, 49; indicators of, 48; luxury goods and, 48–49. *See also* circular economy
edible computing, 100
emotions, 8
Emperial Nation, ix
end of the world: amulets for, 8; movies and, 5; predictions for, 14
Energy Floors, 95
environmental consciousness, 65
episodic memory, 13
Extra Future Store, 97
eyeglasses, 93

fake clothing: Christie's auction house and, 19–20, 23; lookalikes and, 31; Metropolitan Museum and, 24; organic cotton and, 78
FAO. *See* Food and Agriculture Organization
farm-to-table, 72, 80
fashion industry: animal skins and, 33; Hurricane Katrina and, 33; recycled clothing and, 58–59
feathers, xi–xii
Ferragni, Chiara, 105
financial modeling industry, 4
Financial Times, 1
Fisher, Roger, 16
Fitbit, 39
fitness, 40
Food and Agriculture Organization (FAO), 80
food insecurity, 81

foraging cuisine: McCandless and, 69–70; at Noma, 69; pollution and, 71; problems with, 83; return to nature and, 72
forgery, 30, 32
Fortunoff, 2
fracking. *See* hydraulic fracturing
France, 106–7
Fredericks, Brad, 29
Freecycle.org, 51–52
Freemeets: consumer consumption at, 56; Freecycle and, 52; luxury goods and, 57
frivolous spending, 47, 48
Frost, Pat, 21
Funders and Founders, 11

Galton, Francis, 6
Geiser, Bill, 101
gender gap, 47–49
genetically modified crops (GMOs), 79–80
Getting to Yes (Fisher and Ury), 16
Glasser, Michael, 30
global positions system (GPS), 94, 97
Glynn, Cormac, 2
GMO. *See* genetically modified crops
The God Species (Lynas), 82
Google, 90
Gore, Al, 40
Gorman, Paul, 25
Gottlieb, Alma, 115
Goyard, 43
GPS. *See* global positions system
graffiti artist, x
Gramlich, Ed, 34
Green, Marc, 91
Gurley, Bill, 35

ABOUT THE AUTHOR

SYL TANG is CEO and founder of HipGuide Inc. A futurist, her focus is how and why we consume, with an eye toward world events such as natural disasters, geopolitical clashes, and pandemics. She has written hundreds of articles predicting and documenting trends for the *Financial Times*.

Her brand consulting work is behind the launches of some of the most well-known beauty, beverage, automotive, and urban development efforts, including category changers such as frozen alcohol and mineral makeup. Her company HipGuide is a case study taught in universities around the world.